SCIENTIFIC AMERICAN EXPLORES BIG IDEAS

The Science of Pain

The Editors of *Scientific American*

SCIENTIFIC AMERICAN | EDUCATIONAL PUBLISHING

New York

Published in 2027 by Scientific American Educational Publishing
in association with **The Rosen Publishing Group**
2544 Clinton Street, Buffalo NY 14224

Contains material from Scientific American®, a division of Springer Nature America, Inc., reprinted by permission, as well as original material from The Rosen Publishing Group®.

First Edition

Scientific American
Lisa Pallatroni: Project Editor

Rosen Publishing
Nicole Horning: Compiling Editor
Michael Moy: Senior Graphic Designer

Cataloging-in-Publication Data
Names: Scientific American, Inc.
Title: The science of pain / edited by the Scientific American Editors.
Description: Buffalo, New York : Scientific American Educational Publishing, an imprint of Rosen Publishing, 2027. | Series: Scientific American explores big ideas | Includes glossary and index. Identifiers: ISBN 9781538314678 (pbk.) | ISBN 9781538314685 (library bound) | ISBN 9781538314692 (ebook)
Subjects: LCSH: Pain perception–Juvenile literature. | Pain–Physiological aspects–Juvenile literature. | Pain–Treatment–Juvenile literature.
Classification: LCC RB127.S356 2027 | DDC 152.1824–dc23

Manufactured in the United States of America
Websites listed were live at the time of publication.

Cover: PeopleImages/Shutterstock.com

CPSIA Compliance Information: Batch # CS27SA.
For Further Information contact Rosen Publishing at 1-800-237-9932.

CONTENTS

INTRODUCTION

Pain is something everyone experiences. But what exactly is pain? Why does it feel so different from one person to another? From a scraped knee to a chronic pain and other long-term conditions, pain can be sharp, dull, sudden, or constant. It can protect us by warning us of injury, but it can also become a condition of its own that affects daily life.

Pain is the body's way of sending a message. When something goes wrong, like touching a hot surface or twisting an ankle, signals travel through the nervous system to the brain, which interprets them as pain. This process helps us react quickly and avoid further harm. But pain is not just physical. Emotions, past experiences, stress, and even expectations can influence how pain is felt, making it a personal experience that can vary from person to person.

In this book, you'll learn more about the science behind pain and the human body. In Origins of Pain, you'll learn how pain begins, from the moment the body detects injury to how signals are processed in the brain. From there, you'll learn more about why people experience pain differently and how things like mood, memory, and environment can impact pain in The Unique Experience of Pain. In Pain Disorders, you'll explore conditions in which pain persists or occurs without a clear cause, affecting millions of people around the world. Healing Pain and Injuries focuses on how the body repairs itself and the methods used to support recovery. Finally, Pain Relievers and How They Work explores pain medications, how they work, and alternatives to addictive opioid pain relievers.

The study of pain reveals how connected the body and brain are. What starts as a physical signal can be influenced by many different factors, showing that pain is not only a symptom, but an important part of how we experience things. As research continues to grow, scientists and healthcare providers are finding new ways to study, treat, and reduce pain, improving quality of life for people everywhere.

Section 1: Origins of Pain

The Science of Pain

By Steve Mirsky

Welcome to *Science Talk*, the weekly podcast of *Scientific American* for the seven days starting December 3, 2008, I'm Steve Mirsky. If you hate pain, you'll love this week's program. We will talk with pain expert Sean Mackey. Plus, we will test your knowledge about some recent science in the news.

A few weeks back I was at a conference for journalists called Science Writers 2008 at Stanford University. One of the speakers was Sean Mackey. He is a former engineer who then went to med school and is now associate professor and chief of the pain management division of the Stanford University Medical Center. He is also the director of the Stanford Systems Neuroscience and Pain Lab. He gave a talk about pain after which daily podcast contributor Corinna Wu and I double-teamed an interview with Mackey. First, I want to play a few minutes of his talk having to do with pain and empathy, after which we will go right to the conversation with Corinna, me and Mackey.

Mackey: I am also intrigued by this answer to the empathy. It has been verbally defined. One definition is: the observation of an action or perception or emotional state in an individual that activates a corresponding representation in the observer. Let me give you a down-to-earth example, and this is what primarily motivated me in this. I have an 11-year-old son now. He was five at the time that this all started. I was picking him up at day care and he was running across the linoleum floor to come and give me a big hug and he was running too fast; he is a big physical kid and he fell down on his knees and he slid across the linoleum floor, hit his head right into the wall and down stalled. And you could have heard this gasp through the room, just like what you did. There was a huge gasp from all the parents. So I went over and checked his head and he had this huge goose bump, you know, huge tomato growing on his head; I was just making sure he didn't need to go see a neurosurgeon, he didn't have a step-up and he didn't. So [I] high-fived him and said, "Way to go" and he laughed, and we had a good laugh, and I realized at that moment that hurt me more than it hurt him. That hurt me a lot more than it hurt him, and I was asking myself, "Did I just experience brain activity in the same areas of my brain in seeing it happening as he did in actually experiencing it?." So I came back and decided to study it. So we hypothesize that when you see somebody in pain, that you engage the same brain areas as if you experience[d] it yourself; that, we believe, is the fundamental basis of empathy, so what we did is we applied a noxious stimulus to subjects and then we got onto these underground Web sites and we found a variety of different videos that showed things like that.

Steve: At this point, Mackey showed some really unpleasant videos from football games, the kind where a guy's leg is bending in a direction it's really not supposed to go, things like that.

Mackey: I'm sorry. I was supposed to warn you. (laughs) Let's see that again. How many of you felt that? Okay. There is always a number of people in audience that feels that in their ankle also and the intriguing thing about that is that those of you have feel it in their ankles are people who have had prior ankle injury. I think this is another one here.

Steve: That can't be good. You are not going to show Joe Theismann, are you? (laughs)

Mackey: So the gentleman here just asked that if we were going [show] to Joe Theismann, that's a great question; and you know what, we decided not to use Joe Theismann, why?

Steve: It's too much to bear.

Mackey: Ah! It's too much for you, but the thing is it turns out that Joe Theismann's clip is the most showed sports clip, I think, in the history. Too many people have seen it, they have become desensitized; but I got to tell you, we just published two papers on this. I mean, they just came out and in one of the papers we opened up describing the Joe Theismann clip—you know, so if you go and look at our paper, we'll be happy to send it to you—we opened up describing that Joe Theismann clip, how people felt about it afterwards.

Voice: I want to see; what's the clip about?

Mackey: Oh! It shows Joe Theismann getting a compound fracture of his leg, just being crushed. I can't remember who whacked him.

Steve: Lawrence Taylor.

Mackey: Lawrence Taylor just took him out. It was just an extraordinarily violent hit. He was a former quarterback.

Voice: How long ago was that approximately?

Steve: Twenty years ago.

Mackey: Yeah. It was just in the '80s.

Steve: Yeah.

Mackey: I think it took place in the '80s, but it left an indelible mark on everybody who watched football. I mean, they all felt that and it was played over and over and over again. So we elected not to do this. What we found is that indeed the same areas the brain involved with experiencing pain are involved with seeing other people in pain. It was a tremendous overlap, particularly in these emotional and cognitive areas of the brain.

Mackey: This concept of empathy is constructed, it binds all of us in society that when we see somebody in distress that we similarly feel that persons' distress and we want to reach out and help that person. It is an area of tremendous interest in the research community and we want to better understand, what are the neurophysiologic underpinnings of this. In other words, what's going on our brains when we see somebody who is in distress, somebody who is in pain? And so that was part of the motivation for this. I think I related a story about my son, having an injury and my experiencing his pain probably [to] a greater extent than he experienced it himself and that clearly was also a motivator. So we set out. This was a collaboration working with Kevin Ochsner who is now at Columbia University and Kevin is a wonderful neuroscientist who played a key role in running this study and looking inside the brains of people to understand what happens when we see somebody in pain and compare that against when we experience that pain ourselves.

Corinna: So can you tell me about the study? How did you conduct it, how many people did you look at?

Mackey: We looked at two different aspects of the study, one in which people were experiencing pain themselves; and so what we do is we take healthy volunteers and we apply a noxious–in other words, a painful–thermal stimulus to their arm and we give it at such a temperature that it works out to about a [seven out of 10] pain that they are experiencing on their arm, where 0 is no pain and 10 is the worst pain imaginable. And then what we also do is we give them a series of videos that we show people in traumatic and painful events, things where they are breaking their arms, breaking their legs, usually sporting-type injuries. And we've now all seen these; when we did the study, we had to go on to these underground Web sites to be able to mine them. And then what we do is we have them experience pain and then in a separate time during the scanning session, we show them these videos and we are scanning their brain during the whole period of time and we look at the areas that are unique to pain, when you are experiencing it yourself and then also when you are seeing somebody else in pain.

Corinna: And what did you find?

Mackey: Well what we found is that there is a tremendous amount of overlap in those brain regions involved with both the experience of your own pain as well as when you're seeing somebody else experience pain and those brain regions are areas like the anterior insular cortex. This is an area that's involved with interoception, kind of our internal state of bodily awareness. So, when we are self-monitoring, how we're feeling about something, that's an area that's heavily activated and engaged. Also the anterior singular cortex was heavily engaged in both of these conditions, such that this is an area involved with emotional processing, attentional processing and also correcting errors when we are experiencing something that doesn't feel quite right and we need to do something about it. So these areas were both overlapping and engaged with both of these conditions. We also found similar areas and some of the frontal cortical regions involved with our own experience of pain and then seeing somebody else in pain; but there were also some unique areas that ultimately we were able to tease [a]part in our studies. So, pain itself tended to engage more of the sensory systems of the brain, areas like the somatosensory cortex that is engaged whenever you have an acute pain stimulus. Also some of the brainstem regions that have been found to be involved within inhibition of pain, so that when we, for instance, we are distracted away from an event or when we're trying to turn down internal bodily pain, those descending systems tend to get engaged; and we found that was more unique for own experience of pain that we saw somebody else in pain.

Corinna: And how would we as humans benefit from being able to empathize somebody else's pain?

Mackey: Oh! I think without empathy, you know, my senses probably would have died out as a species a long time ago. Think about it. If we didn't come to the rescue of those who were in distress, those that we loved, people would have just died. So it is this construct that binds all of us in society. So I think empathy is extraordinarily important and it's something that has developed through, you know, mammalian evolution and is extraordinarily beneficial to all of us, and I think it's the absence of empathy, when we run into the problems that we see in society. So, you know, the absolute absence of empathy, you know, we run into sociopaths and psychopaths. People who don't engage that empathic response, who don't have those feelings when they see somebody who is in pain and we can all point at people through history that are examples of what has happened when there has been a total lack of empathy and those people are in positions of power.

Corinna: And you mentioned there was one subject in your study or, person in your study, who actually showed no response, is that right?

Mackey: Yes. So as a side note, we had one subject who didn't show much in the way of brain activity at all to these painful videos and we went back and interviewed that subject and found out that he was an ex-convict. Now, you know, I'm careful about drawing any conclusions about that in a more global state and those types of things need to studied more systematically, but I think it is an intriguing finding.

Corinna: I mean, does that suggest, I mean, some kind of diagnostic value to, you know, seeing if someone can empathize with another?

Mackey: And I want to be real careful about extending our findings our any other people's findings to using fMRI or imaging as a diagnostic test in 2008. We're still a long way away from that, and I mention that with such strong emphasis because I'm becoming more and more concerned about the use of neuroimaging tools being used inappropriately as diagnostic tests in the medical field as well as in the legal field, in trying to determine does this person have pain, does this person have a psychiatric condition? I think we're a still long way away from being able to use it in that context.

Corinna: Are there further studies that you are planning in this to investigate this?

Mackey: So we are looking at ranges of empathy in people and being able to characterize empathetic responses within those groups of people; and then also there has been some recent discussions about people with spinal cord injury, for instance, and whether or not you need to have incoming sensory input from the body to be able to actually engage an empathic response. And so there has been some discussions in our group about going down that direction because that might actually help provide additional information as to these neurophysiologic underpinnings of empathy.

Steve: That's really interesting because it gets into, you know, how much a robot could ever be like a human; or well, how much does a human who has lost mobility still fully– I don't mean to denigrate paraplegics–but how much is their experience of, you know, their sensory experience, how much is that now divorced from humanity as well?

Mackey: Yes, where this came up is I've got both some friends as well as patients that I [take] care of that have spinal cord injuries, high spinal cord injuries, and I have simply asked them, you know, can you compare and contrast before your injury and after your injury when you see somebody in a traumatic situation, in a situation in which you are experiencing pain, does your response to it change? And at least anecdotally they've just suggested that, yes, they are not getting that kicked in the gut feeling that they used to get before the injury. Now I got to tell you, that's a long way away from actually having definitive results, but at least it helps us pose additional questions to understand it.

Steve: I wanted to talk about the brain's reaction to pain. Over the last couple of decades there has been a growing realization that you don't just experience pain, your brain actually rewires your whole nervous system as a reaction to it that can be permanent. And can you tell us something about what's going on in the brain as we experience pain, especially chronic pain?

Mackey: So we've now all heard of this concept of neuroplasticity, this idea of the changing brain, the concept of networks and neurons rewiring and changing their function in the face of chronic pain; and we're beginning to appreciate that this area of neuroplasticity is important not only in perhaps causing pain, but also in maintaining pain and that, you know, patients with chronic pain, these neuroplastic changes that occur are not turning off. Let me take a step back. We know that even in an acute situation, that in an acute pain situation we get neuroplasticity. We get changes within the spinal cord in the brain even after an acute injury and it happens in each and every one of us. We sprain an ankle, we cut our hand, after a period of time, over period of hours of a course of the day, we get neuroplastic changes and it sends a signal to us to protect that injured limb; and it's highly beneficial because if we didn't have that message, that signal, that behavior that was being generated, we would go out and continue to injure that limb over and over again. Now in a normal situation, those factors that cause the plasticity turn off and the limb is perceived as being healthy and normal again. In a chronic pain situations, those neural switches are not turning off and we believe that they are continuing to grow, continuing to expand; and in many cases, expanding well beyond the area that was originally injured, encompassing other limbs. And we think that that is playing a role in conditions like fibromyalgia and other conditions that involve global, widespread pain. There have been studies in which brain atrophy has been looked at in fibromyalgia patient[s]. Cathy Bushnell did a lovely study, and elegant study looking at changes with the brain in the singular cortex in the parahippocampal gyrus, which is involved with a stress response and showing shrinkage of the brain. Vania Apkarian did [an] elegant study looking at low-back pain patients and showing changes in prefrontal cortical regions of the brain and insular cortical as well as anterior singular cortex areas of the brain involved with low-back pain. What was most intriguing about his study is that the prefrontal regions of the brain that were shown to shrink were also the same areas that are engaged in things like working memory. (This is what used to be referred to as short-term memory.) And so once again, maybe these cognitive deficits that our patients are experiencing in the face of chronic pain, maybe they are not due to the medications we put people on; maybe it's not just due to depression, maybe it's due to the chronic pain itself that's causing this rewiring within the brain. Now the question comes up: What do these brain changes really represent? What does shrinkage in the brain represent? And the truth is we don't know the answer yet. We have some intriguing guidance from the depression literature in which they've done autopsy studies in people who were scanned before passing away, and they did biopsies of the brain. What they found, at least in depression, was that it wasn't neuronal cell loss that was accounting for the brain shrinkage; it was loss of glial cells, these supporting cells that are now getting a tremendous amount of attention in the area of pain, as well as other disease conditions. Now, we still need to do those types of studies in pain, but at least it gives us some guidance as to what may be going on. The follow up question to that would be: "Can we reverse these changes? Can we actually turn back the clock? Can we turn back the changes in the brain to something in a more normal situation?" And we don't have the date on that yet. Our group is running studies to look at whether those changes are reversible. Other groups are also running this, and we're all hoping that with appropriate therapy not only can we reduce the pain and suffering in our patients and its impact on society, but that we will have objective measures within the brain to correlate with those changes.

Steve: Does this work imply that we should really be more aggressive in pain right at its outset?

Mackey: Absolutely. We realize more and more that it's better to prevent the pain rather than to try to treat it after the fact, rather than trying to get that horses who has already left the barn. And there are a number of studies now that show the preventative measures can have a big impact in reducing the number of people who go on to have chronic pain.

Steve: There is a virtue, I think, there is a cultural kind of virtue in gutting it out rather than taking medications; and should we just, should we get past that and just start popping those Advils as soon as you sprain your ankle?

Mackey: There is this message in society [that] we do have to suck it up, that we do have to tough out the pain; in that, you know, we are a better person as a consequence if we do so and there is some truth to having the internal tenacity to dealing with the pain and continuing to work in the face of pain. However, I want to separate that from the idea of appropriately treating the pain in an acute situation and making sure that we're doing everything we can to prevent that acute pain episode from going on to being one that's more chronic. What we're trying to figure out right now is why, for a given person, the vast number of people who have surgery in our society or who have an injury, why do the vast number of those people go on and heal perfectly well, who have no chronic pain afterwards; but there is a subset of people who do go onto have for a given injury longstanding chronic pain issues? We know that some of those issues are related to genetic differences, you know, and we can't choose unfortunately our parents and the genes they've passed down to us, but we can change some of the environmental influences. And so we're trying to understand both those genetic factors as well as the environmental factors that go on to cause somebody to have chronic pain after an injury or after a surgery and then being able to focus the treatments that can ultimately reduce that incidence of chronic pain; and then hopefully also the amount of medications that people need to use after surgery. Because we're seeing just an epidemic of prescription opioid use in our society. You know, we look at Vicodin, which I believe is prescribed to 135 million times in America alone–I think it's the most prescribed medication in society. You know, we're seeing this medication use more and more and more, and we want to make sure it's being used appropriately; but we know that they are a number of people who go onto misuse these medications and abuse these medications and so this is where pain is very tightly linked with this idea of addiction and addiction to prescription opioids, and that's why we need to do a better job in figuring out who are the people that are going to go on to have chronic pain, who are the people that are going to go on and use these prescription opioids and put the appropriate treatments in place.

Steve: Our opioids, especially in, say, postsurgical situations, are they still sometimes under-utilized though, leading to this next stage where somebody weeks later might then be on them and wind up abusing them?

Mackey: Yes, so there are arguments about using these medications earlier rather than later, to try to stamp out the pain early on rather than try to deal with it afterwards; and opioids play a very useful part of that treatment. There are now other medications that we've learnt that can also be very effective in that acute setting. The typical things that people are used to hearing about things like nonsteroidal anti-inflammatories, the ibuprofen, the Naprosyn, the Tylenols; but there is[are] also new medications that have been used in the acute pain setting that have also been found to reduce pain after surgery; and things like the gabapentinoids–which go under the name gabapentin or pregabalin–have been shown to be very effective in that postsurgical period of time. Now, these medications are used off label, but the studies are showing time and time again that they've been very effective for the treatment of acute pain.

Steve: Big places–like Stanford, like Sloane-Kettering in New York–have established pain centers, so how, though, has this idea that pain [is] its own condition, how has that translated to society at large to this point?

Mackey: Well, I think first of all, it has helped a lot of patients from [a] validation standpoint; to recognize that pain is a disease in and of it's own has helped patients that have been suffering in silence, that have been desperate for some degree of validation of their pain problem; and has given them some sense of security and some sense of confidence so they can go out now and seek better treatment. Because the problem with pain ultimately, with chronic pain, is that they still have pain despite the fact that the tissue has healed. And so often times there is no obvious source or site of the pain, but these people are still suffering. And so I think recognizing the pain as a disease in its own right has gone a long way from a patient's standpoint. It's also gone a long way from a government and a societal standpoint in helping to allocate resources. And so we've recently just seen new bills that have been passed by Congress that have allocated moneys towards the VA–and I think very appropriately so–to our veterans who are coming back from Iraq, who are just experiencing horrific injuries, and many of whom unfortunately will have chronic pain problems. And so I am very pleased to see that Congress has been allocating funds and resources from more research in that area. Where we need to be taking the next step is to be recognizing it from an overall societal standpoint. We need to be able to delegate more moneys towards the NIH to deal with this problem of chronic pain and not only just pain, but see the overlap that pain has with all of these other conditions that we face in society. Because in many of these situations, we find it is not the disease state itself that's causing the disability, the loss of work productivity. It's the pain that is doing that, and if we can do a better job with the pain, we would often find that the patients are going back to work earlier. They are using less medical resources and ultimately we end up spending less, not more.

Steve: Well, that's an [investment], that's not overhead, because your productivity would [go] way up, nationwide.

Mackey: Oh, indeed. And I think you've seen the large companies start to invest in these early-prevention programs trying to recognize those workers who are more likely to go on and have a chronic pain problem and who are more likely to file a worker's compensation claim, intervene early, get them their help that they need so that they don't end up losing a very productive worker.

Corinna: I am just curious to know how you went from electrical engineering to neuroscience.

Mackey: You know you could not have come across a more linear, in the box, kind of guy than me when I was in electrical engineering, and even when I was early on in medical school. If you had come to me and talk with me about things like the placebo effect or acupuncture or meditation, I would have been asking you, "What were you smoking?" I was a believer in the biomedical model that you find the disease, you find the source of injury or pathology, you give the pill, you reverse the condition and the person is cured. And it took me a long time to realize just how terribly wrong I was. I learned that through spending time with patients. In working in the pain clinic and seeing that it wasn't so much that the injection, the needle, the procedure, the pill that I was giving them that was making them better. It was actually talking with them. It was understanding their painful condition, where were they coming from and what were the factors that were influencing their pain, and it was important then that that we may need to understand that. Because at my core I am still an engineer, but I decided to apply that to the brain, because that's ultimately the seat of who we are. And so all of these factors that go on to change a person's experience has some neural basis within the brain, and so for me, it's an obvious link. It took me a long time to get here, but I think that I am a much better as a consequence for having gone down that path and hopefully will be able to contribute somewhat to answering some of these questions.

Steve: What motivated you to go to medical school in the first place then?

Mackey: Oh, I think I am an example [of] that old phrase, "You are who hang with", so I always enjoyed both the sciences as well as medicine, and I had a number of friends and mentors who were MD-PhDs in engineering and in medicine and I naturally gravitated towards them, not realizing that you know, we are fairly a small group of people. But while it was uncommon back in the '80s and '90s when I was doing my training, I think we are seeing it becoming more and more common as we see this intersection between technology, engineering, physics and medicine and healthcare, and I think we are going to see more and more people go into this field, and I think we need more people to go into this field. If at the very least, not necessarily to do research in engineering, pure engineering or pure physics, but to act as a bridge between those people who do the engineering and the physics work and health care. So I don't do pure engineering research anymore. I long ago had to give that up. Fortunately, there are a just absolutely amazing engineers here on campus that do that work, and where I fit in is acting as a bridge to be able to communicate the healthcare concepts to them and then take it from them back to my other medical colleagues.

Steve: Especially with more and more bionics coming into play, that's going to be crucial.

Mackey: Oh, [it's] an exciting time. The area of bionics and brain-computer interfaces. It is just an exciting time to be alive and it's an exciting time to be doing research in this area.

Steve: One of the other writers who attended Mackey's talk has a nice summary of his entire presentation; you can find it at www.sciencegeekgirl.wordpress.com/2008/10; and Mackey's Web site is paincenter.stanford.edu

(music)

Steve: Now its time to play TOTALL...... Y BOGUS. Here are four science stories, but only three are true. See if you know which story is TOTALL...... Y BOGUS.

Story number 1: If you feel physically clean, you will probably judge other people more leniently.

Story number 2: It's bad today, but greenhouse gas carbon dioxide may have saved the ancient earth from becoming completely covered with ice.

Story number 3: A species of sea slug, an animal, can carry out photosynthesis.

And story number 4: Researching your medical symptoms on the Web, on average, gets you as good a diagnosis as seeing a general practitioner.

Time is up.

Story 1 is true. Feeling physically clean reduces the severity of moral judgment. That's according to research published in the journal *Psychological Science*. Study subjects watched a film clip categorized by the researchers as disgusting but some washed their hands just before viewing their film and they were less offended by the film.

Story 2 is true. It looks like carbon dioxide kept the Earth from becoming an ice ball in the Cryogenian period about 842 [million] to 635 million years ago. That research appears in the latest issue of the *Nature Geoscience*. This view is contrary to the snowball Earth hypothesis, which says that the planet was indeed iced over. The new study says that as the temperature got lower, the ocean water absorbed more oxygen, which broke down organic matter, which released carbon dioxide which started warming things up again.

And story 3 is true. The sea slug is an animal but it can carry on photosynthesis. It basically steals the machinery for doing so from algae and then runs it in its own body for up to nine months, converting light to energy. For more check out the December 1st edition of the daily *SciAm* podcast, *60-Second Science*.

All of which means that story 4, about researching medical conditions on the Web leading to accurate diagnosis, is TOTALL...... Y BOGUS, because what is true is that your far more likely to find zebras rather than horses when you search for your particular health prints. The first study of health-related Web searches found that worst case scenarios come up most often. The sites are more popular and thus get ranked highest by Google algorithms. So on the Web, your chest pain is much more likely to be heart attack than heartburn. For more, check out the December 2nd episode of our neuroscience and psychology podcast, *60-Second Pysch*.

Well that's it for this edition of *Scientific American's Science Talk*. Visit http://www.SciAm.com for all the latest science news, and check out our In-Depth Report this week on HIV and AIDS. For Science Talk, I'm Steve Mirsky. Thanks for clicking on us.

About the Author

Steve Mirsky was the winner of a Twist contest in 1962, for which he received three crayons and three pieces of construction paper. It remains his most prestigious award.

The Chronification of Pain

By Daniel Barron

Earlier this year, I wrote about my patient, Andrew, an engineer who developed a heroin habit. An unfortunate series of joint replacements had left Andrew with terrible pain and, when his medication ran out, he turned to heroin.

Months after his surgeries—after his tissue and scars had healed—Andrew remained disabled by a deep, biting pain. I recall puzzling over his pain, how it had spread throughout his body and how previous clinical teams had prescribed progressively higher doses of opioids to tame it.

Andrew had transitioned from acute pain (i.e., pain from his surgical wounds) to chronic pain (i.e., pain in the absence of an obvious cause), but it was unclear to me whether this reflected a drug tolerance or a different pain process.

Drug Tolerance and Chronic Pain

The difference between drug tolerance and chronic pain is a difficult concept to get hold of. In the hospital workroom one morning, I realized how confused I was by the topic and paged the hospital's on-call pain specialist. Fortune smiled and Donna-Ann M Thomas, Yale University's Pain Medicine Division Chief, picked up the phone and patiently explained how tolerance and chronic pain are quite different.

Andrew became tolerant to opioids when his body required progressively larger doses to have the same effect. Opioids activate the *Mu* opioid receptor, which blocks pain signals in the spinal cord. To find a way around the opioid blockade, Andrew's body had made more *Mu* receptors to compensate for the drug, meaning more drug had to be present to stifle the pain signal, hence the escalating doses.

Chronic pain, Thomas explained, differs from tolerance and even acute pain. In Andrew's case, chronic pain was the agony he felt weeks after one of his (many) surgeries, despite the fact that his body had healed and was no longer sending distress signals from his joint, through his spinal cord.

The Purpose and Problem of Pain

Your body has a system of neurons and neural pathways whose sole purpose is to detect pain and transmit painful signals. Specialized subsets of neurons are devoted to specific forms of pain, such as pain caused by heat, or chemicals, or cuts. Pain is a serious matter. Your brain carefully monitors for threats in the environment and, should you accidently touch a hot stove, for example, your pain system seizes your attention and throws your cognitive machinery into red alert. You yank your hand away Your emotions are riled up–"Who left the damn stove on?" Maybe you cry a little. Maybe you're in a bad mood for a while.

The goal isn't to create a moody panic, but rather to mobilize your brain's learning, memory and decision-making systems. The purpose of pain is to associate an environmental threat with a strongly negative emotion and to demand a course correction away from whatever caused that painful signal. In this sense, pain is a useful alarm–a lighthouse that keeps you from more serious trouble.

The problem is that, like any machine, the brain is vulnerable to errors: if a response to pain is learned, it might be learned incorrectly. Or the alarm might never shut off.

So why does pain transition from acute to chronic? A traditional view is that the more severe an acute injury, the more likely the pain will linger–like the way hitting a cymbal with a hard, heavy mallet creates an enduring *crash*. And yet it could also be that the cymbal itself, once struck, somehow sustains its own *ostinato*. Is the problem the mallet or the cymbal?

Chronic Back Pain

The neuroscience question is whether the brains of people who develop chronic pain (known as pain chronification) differ from those who don't and whether this difference is detectable before or after pain chronification.

To answer the question, a group of neuroscientists led by A. Vania Apkarian at Northwestern University followed a group of thirty-nine patients who had injured their backs.

For three years, Apkarian used M.R.I. to gather incremental measures of the structure and function of patients' brains. The goal was to see how and whether the brain changes during pain chronification and whether the brains of people who transition from acute to chronic pain differed from those whose pain resolved.

Apkarian's group had shown that the corticolimbic network was involved. The corticolimbic system includes the medial prefrontal cortex, nucleus accumbens, hippocampus, and amygdala; structures associated with cognitive processes like judgment, motivation, memory, and emotion. Previous research from Apkarian's lab had used functional M.R.I. to show that strong functional connections between the nucleus accumbens and the medial prefrontal cortex prospectively predict pain chronification. To follow-up this study, they wanted to know whether the brain's structure also prospectively predicted patients who would develop chronic pain.

What they discovered was surprising: the presence of pain does not restructure the corticolimbic network. Rather, even before the onset of back pain, the corticolimic network was more densely connected in patients who developed chronic pain than in patients who did not. In addition, patients with smaller hippocampi and amygdalae–structures with strong genetic dependence implicated in emotional learning, anxiety, and stress regulation–were also more likely to develop chronic pain.

Together, these observations suggest that some intrinsic, genetically encoded brain property–and not the pain itself–led to chronic pain. The cymbal, not the mallet, was the culprit.

The implication of Akparian's work is that a patient's risk of pain chronification can be measured and therefore clinically managed. For patients like Andrew, it could mean the difference between properly managed pain chronification and a crescendo into opioid tolerance and heroin.

About the Author

Daniel Barron is director of the Pain Intervention and Digital Research Program, a National Institutes of Health–funded research clinic devoted to developing better tools to define chronic pain and psychiatric conditions, at Brigham and Women's Hospital and Spaulding Rehabilitation Hospital. He completed his medical training and psychiatry residency at Yale University, his graduate work at the University of Texas and his fellowship in interventional pain medicine at the University of Washington. He is author of Reading Our Minds: The Rise of Big Data Psychiatry. *Follow him on X (formerly Twitter) @daniel__barron or visit his website at danielsbarron.com*

Nerve Damage Might Explain Chronic Pain

By Stephani Sutherland

Deborah Reed lived in a tall historic house on a tree-lined street in tony northwest Portland, Ore. In 2003 the author and mother of two boys developed deep muscle pain and profound fatigue, seemingly out of nowhere. "I remember climbing the wood stairs to my bedroom on the third floor," Reed recalls. "It was agonizing." Reed would spend entire days in her bed, getting up only for trips to the bathroom. When the pain was at its worst, she once went 10 days without leaving her bedroom.

Her doctor suspected depression and explained to Reed that pain can accompany that ailment. "But I just knew that's not what this was," she says. "This was something else." In addition to widespread muscle aches, Reed experienced tingling and burning sensations in her hands and feet, headaches, and painful sensitivity to temperature and light touch. Specialists tested Reed for multiple sclerosis, arthritis, cancer, lupus, Lyme disease and a catalogue of autoimmune conditions to no avail. After two years of evaluation, a rheumatologist finally gave Reed a diagnosis: fibromyalgia.

For her, like many others, the diagnosis left many questions unanswered. An estimated five million Americans are believed to have fibromyalgia, the vast majority of them women. Physicians do not call fibromyalgia a disease, however. They diagnose this syndrome when they encounter a collection of pain symptoms for which they have ruled out all other potential causes. Most often these symptoms include deep muscle pain that affects the whole body, a flulike, achy feeling and fatigue.

Physicians first identified this bundle of symptoms more than a century ago, but research languished until 1977, when scientists at the University of Toronto described the tender and aching symptoms more formally, sparking new interest. By 1990 the American College of Rheumatology had settled on the name "fibromyalgia" and developed guidelines for consistent diagnosis.

At that time rheumatologists were hunting for signs of inflammation or injury in the joints and muscles. The pain of fibromyalgia, after all, seemed to stem from these areas. Yet they came up empty time and again, and in the past 10 years scientists have instead focused largely on the brain. Now, however, some researchers are beginning to suspect that they called off the search for bodily harm too soon. New studies from neurologists working around the world suggest that these unexplained aches might arise at least in part from damaged nerves. If physicians can halt the destruction and heal those wounds, they might also stop the pain.

A Medical Mystery

For Reed, the diagnosis came as a surprise. "I had never heard of fibromyalgia," she says. She quickly realized she was not alone–even some of her doctors were unfamiliar with the condition or doubted its existence. Despite thousands of studies spanning more than 30 years, fibromyalgia remains remarkably mysterious. The severity of symptoms seems to run the gamut: whereas some people experience only mild discomfort or fatigue, others become incapacitated.

Not all pains are equal. Typically pain is good because it alerts you that your body has sustained damage, prompting you to defend yourself against further destruction. Pain becomes chronic when a warning signal persists even after the threat is gone. Fibromyalgia is one of many recognized forms of chronic pain. Most types of long-term pain are considered either inflammatory, as in some types of arthritis, or neuropathic, which often involves nerve damage. Part of the mystery of fibromyalgia is that its symptoms come from both categories, a fact that has only served to frustrate researchers, who have failed to find consistent evidence of either inflammation or damage.

Underlying their bafflement is the conundrum of what causes fibromyalgia. One clue is that fibromyalgia appears to be partly heritable. Genes might account for up to half the risk for it. Researchers now agree that some people inherit a predisposition to chronic pain that springs from differences in genes that encode key pain-signaling molecules. Yet the genetic risk factors linked with fibromyalgia are not limited to pain-related circuitry. Some of the same quirks of the genetic code also crop up with depression and anxiety disorders.

The psychological history of fibromyalgia patients further deepens the riddle. For example, it often develops after physical or emotional trauma. Experts now suspect that fibromyalgia occurs when individuals with an inherited risk are exposed to a physiological trigger, whether from illness, injury or a psychological crisis. "One could imagine a combination of genetic predeterminants that could tip people toward pain," says neurologist Claudia Sommer of the University of Würzburg in Germany. "If you have a happy life, you might tolerate this well, but if catastrophes come along, they could tip you over to chronic pain." Reed, for one, traces her symptoms to a serious head-on car collision she suffered about a year before her troubles developed.

The question of how such varied incidents trigger full-blown fibromyalgia still stumps researchers. Some physicians even suspect the syndrome is actually a collection of separate but similar ailments. Despite these unknowns, the diagnosis brings some comfort to patients like Reed, who found it tremendously helpful to name her pain, discover people with similar symptoms and be taken seriously by her doctor. "To be able to know, okay, I'm not crazy–it was such a relief," she says.

Brain's Pains

To make sense of some of fibromyalgia's brain-based symptoms–such as fatigue, memory problems and sleep disturbance–researchers have used imaging to explore whether fibromyalgia patients process pain differently than healthy people. They have found that people with this syndrome appear to have less brain volume in the cingulate cortex and the medial frontal cortex, areas thought to be critical to our overall experience of pain. Other research points to altered activity in brain areas dedicated to attention and the processing of sensory input, such as sound. Scientists hypothesize that the brain's "volume control" for such sensations may be off-kilter, potentially magnifying pain.

These insights have helped shape the therapeutic approach to treating fibromyalgia, which has focused overwhelmingly on the brain. The only three drugs approved by the U.S. Food and Drug Administration to treat fibromyalgia are an anticonvulsant and two antidepressant medications. These serotonin and norepinephrine reuptake inhibitors, or SNRIs, are thought to dampen pain signals in the brain and spinal cord.

Yet they fail to restore most fibromyalgia patients to health. Reviews published in 2012 and 2013 concluded that the drugs provide modest pain relief for some patients but do not improve sleep or overall quality of life. Moreover, none of these findings clarified whether fibromyalgia changes the brain or whether some patients' brains are prewired for chronic pain. Although the patterns seen in the brains of fibromyalgia patients were initially hailed as hallmarks of the syndrome, these signatures have turned out to be common across chronic pain conditions. Researchers now suspect that the experience of chronic pain actually reshapes the brain's architecture and activity patterns, just as learning to ride a bike or speak a new language would.

Clues from the Periphery

Meanwhile nerve specialists in Germany, Boston and Spain had noticed a peculiar pattern in patients diagnosed with small-fiber polyneuropathy (SFPN), a pain condition that stems from damage to peripheral nerves. Many SFPN patients had previously received the fibromyalgia label.

One of those neurologists, Anne Louise Oaklander of Massachusetts General Hospital, began seeking collaborators to investigate the link, but she could not find a rheumatologist willing to embark on such a speculative, interdisciplinary project. Finally, Oaklander took matters into her own hands. To search for signs of nerve damage in people with fibromyalgia, her team used several tests, including a skin biopsy, in which a clinician punches out a small sample from the skin of the hand or leg and examines the tiny nerves within the sample under a microscope. "No one had really looked appropriately before at nerves," Oaklander says.

The team's findings, published in 2013, revealed a troubling absence of nerve endings in 41 percent of the 27 fibromyalgia patients studied. This is identical to the damage seen in SFPN, in which injury or disease batters nerves until the endings have withered away. In the same year Sommer found comparable results. The new findings were striking: together they suggested that peripheral neuropathy might contribute to fibromyalgia in some patients.

Given the heterogeneous nature of the syndrome, neither Oaklander nor Sommer would expect every patient to show consistent nerve damage. Instead the findings raise the possibility that neuropathy typifies one variant of fibromyalgia. Perhaps the battering sustained by surface-level nerves initiates fibromyalgia's symptoms or, as Sommer suspects, indicates more extensive impairment in nerves serving muscles and tendons. In 2014 two additional reports detected peripheral nerve deterioration in fibromyalgia patients, strengthening the consensus that this damage could play an important role.

Biopsy studies confirmed the appearance of neuropathy but did not reveal how the nerves were acting. Neurologist Jordi Serra of MC Mutua and Neuroscience Technologies, both in Spain, tackled this question using a challenging technique called microneurography, whereby a needlelike electrode is inserted into a skin nerve to record its electrical impulses. Comparing the nerve recordings from healthy individuals with patients with either SFPN or fibromyalgia, Serra's team found that in one third of the pain patients, pain-sensing nerves showed spontaneous, abnormal activity not seen in any control subjects.

The findings, published in 2014 in *Annals of Neurology*, suggest that nerves fire excessively in some SFPN and fibromyalgia patients. "Normally, these nerves are sitting quietly, waiting to detect a burn or pinch, for example," Serra says. But here the pain detectors appear overactive or extra sensitized. It is possible that the same battering that knocked out nerve endings also altered nerve sensitivity. The overactivity, he says, could explain subsequent aches and distress: "Because [these nerves] are hyperexcitable, they discharge spontaneously. These signals go up to the brain, and this is the basis of ongoing pain."

Researchers know that SFPN can be caused by injury, diabetes, genetic mutation or an immune system attack. They therefore hypothesize that similar processes might underlie the nerve loss seen in some fibromyalgia cases. The persistent pain signal would then rewire the nervous system gradually, priming the body for pain. The resemblance to SFPN presents the enticing possibility that by treating the underlying condition, such as an autoimmune disorder, doctors could alleviate or even cure some cases of fibromyalgia.

With the Rain Came Pain

In Portland, where rain drips from the big-leaf maples most months of the year, Reed had noticed that her aches would mostly abate during the warm Oregon summers. But when the temperature dropped below about 55 degrees Fahrenheit and the rain inevitably returned in the fall, so would her discomfort. "That sort of weather change was the most reliable trigger of pain," she remembers.

She and her family would take trips to Mexico every winter to afford her some relief. "As soon as I stepped off the plane into the sun and heat, I could literally feel my body healing. And the opposite happened when I would return to Portland." Eventually Reed moved south to sunny Los Angeles, where she has found her affliction is much more manageable.

Reed's sensitivity to weather and temperature, a feature common to many cases of fibromyalgia, could also relate to nerve anomalies.

In 2013 neuroscientist Frank Rice, then at Albany Medical College, and his colleagues described the nerves that end at tiny blood vessels in the hands, called arteriole-venule shunts, in fibromyalgia patients. These shunts, found near the surface of the palms, increase and decrease blood flow to regulate bodily temperature. They also regulate blood flow to deeper tissues, allowing muscles and organs to function during exercise. Rice found that compared with healthy control subjects, people with the syndrome had significantly more nerve endings at the shunts dedicated to opening blood vessels.

Rice postulates that the disparity in nerve endings might cause shunts to open and close inappropriately, hindering normal heat exchange. Malfunctioning shunts could rob deep muscles and organs of proper blood flow. Muscles deprived of energizing oxygen-rich blood might also contribute to fibromyalgia's hallmark fatigue. For the moment, Rice concedes that we do not know what role shunts play in fibromyalgia, but the anomaly warrants further investigation.

The evidence from Rice and others strongly suggests that fibromyalgia includes components of physical damage or nerve irregularities in a substantial subset of patients. None of the new studies' authors would challenge the idea that fibromyalgia involves real changes in the central nervous system (CNS). Instead they believe that researchers will have the best shot at understanding the condition overall—and at guiding successful future treatments—by studying both its central and peripheral elements.

Cause or Consequence?

Not all scientists agree on the true meaning of the findings about peripheral nerves. Some, such as rheumatologist Daniel Clauw of the University of Michigan, feel strongly that the newly described nerve abnormalities are merely a by-product of an overactive nervous system. "In pain states, we know there is remodeling of the CNS," Clauw says, alluding to the ways that pain, like learning, causes changes in the brain's architecture. "So why wouldn't that likewise occur in the peripheral nervous system?"

Other physicians and researchers, however, see a ray of hope in the new findings. The most effective management strategy, says Roland Staud, who studies and treats fibromyalgia at the University of Florida, addresses both body and mind. Staud recommends exercise, improved sleep habits and cognitive-behavior therapy, which teaches patients mental strategies to cope with their pain. Reed has developed her own routines, which include a healthy diet, yoga and gentle exercise, such as walking and swimming in her L.A. apartment's outdoor pool. And Reed constantly works to minimize stress—another major pain trigger.

Staud is optimistic that for patients who have detectable damage, healing nerves could alleviate the broader symptoms of fibromyalgia. In other neuropathic pain conditions, researchers have found experimentally that blocking an aberrant nerve's overactive signaling with anesthetics can abate even those symptoms rooted in the CNS. In addition, treating possible sources of nerve injury, such as diabetes or immune disorders, helps SFPN patients. Similar approaches might also work for fibromyalgia patients.

Ultimately, our experience of pain culminates in the brain, but it can originate anywhere, from the skin on a big toe to the cortex. The chance to quiet pain signals at any point along the way could alleviate them, so researchers need to consider all possible targets. "I don't pretend that we have solved the mystery of fibromyalgia," Oaklander says. Cracking that case may require teasing apart the many different kinds of patients gathered under the syndrome's label. Yet the clues emerging from patients' nerves might finally allow researchers to start unraveling fibromyalgia's tangle of symptoms and bring relief to millions of patients.

About the Author

Stephani Sutherland is a neuroscientist and science journalist based in southern California. She wrote about the causes of long COVID in our March 2023 issue. Follow her on X @SutherlandPhD

New Culprits in Chronic Pain

By R. Douglas Fields

Helen's left foot slipped off the clutch on impact, twisting her ankle against the car's floorboard. It felt like a minor sprain at the time, she recalls, but the pain never subsided. Instead it intensified. Eventually, the slightest touch, even the gentle brush of bed linen, shot electric flames up her leg. "I was in so much pain I could not speak, yet inside I was screaming," wrote the young Englishwoman in an online journal of the mysterious condition that would torment her for the next three years.

The chronic pain suffered by people like Helen is different from the warning slap of acute pain. Acute pain is the body's most alarming, intense sensation, whose purpose is to stop us from further injuring ourselves. This type of pain is also called pathological pain because an external cause, such as tissue damage, produces the signals that travel the nervous system to the brain, where they are perceived as pain. But imagine if the gut-wrenching agony of a real injury never stopped, even after the wound healed, or if everyday sensations became excruciating: "I was unable to shower ... the water felt like daggers," Helen remembers. "The vibrations in a car, someone walking across floorboards, people talking, a gentle breeze ... would set off the uncontrollable pain. Common painkillers ... even morphine had no effect. It was like my mind was playing tricks on me."

Unfortunately, Helen was right. Her chronic pain stemmed from a malfunction in the body's pain circuits, causing them to continually trigger a false alarm, one that is termed neuropathic because it arises from the misbehavior of the nerves themselves. When the false signals reach the brain, the agony they inflict is as real as any life-threatening pain, yet it never goes away and doctors are often powerless to quiet it.

Recent research is finally elucidating why traditional pain drugs often fail to quell neuropathic pain: the drugs target only neurons when the underlying source of the pain can be the dysfunction of nonneuronal cells called glia that reside in the brain and spinal cord. New insights into how these cells, whose job is to nurture the activity of neurons, can themselves become unbalanced and disrupt neuronal function are sparking new ideas for treating chronic pain. The work is also providing a surprising perspective on an unfortunate corollary of current pain treatment in some people: narcotic addiction.

Pain Circuits and Breakers

Understanding what could cause pain to persist after an injury has healed requires some knowledge of what causes pain at all. Although the sensation of hurt is ultimately perceived in the brain, the nerve cells that produce it are not located there; rather they line the spinal cord, gathering sensory information from throughout the body. Dorsal root ganglion (DRG) neurons, which represent the first stage of a three-part pain-sensing circuit, have their cell bodies stuffed like clusters of grapes in the seam between each vertebra of the backbone, resembling rows of buttons on a double-breasted jacket running from tailbone to skull. Each DRG neuron, like a person with two outstretched arms, extends one slender feeler, known as an axon or fiber, outward to survey a tiny distant region of the body while reaching its other axon into the spinal cord to touch a neuron that will relay impulses through the second stage in pain circuitry, a chain of spinal cord neurons. These spinal pain-transmitting cells in the cord relay messages from DRG neurons up to the final stage, the brain stem and ultimately the cerebral cortex. Pain signals originating from the left side of the body cross inside the spinal cord to travel to the right brain, and signals from the right side are sent to the left brain.

Interrupting the flow of information at any point along the three-stage pain circuit can blunt acute pain. Local anesthetics, such as the Novocain dentists use to painlessly extract a tooth, numb axon tips around the injection site, preventing the cells from firing electrical impulses. A "spinal block," often used to eliminate pain in childbirth, stops pain impulses at the second stage of the circuit, as bundles of DRG cell axons enter the spinal cord to meet spinal neurons. This blockade leaves the mother fully conscious to experience and assist in the painless delivery of her child. A morphine injection works at the same location, reducing transmission of pain signals by spinal neurons while leaving awareness of nonpainful sensations intact. In contrast, general anesthetics used in major surgery disrupt information processing in the cerebral cortex, rendering the patient completely unaware of any sensory input from neural pathways outside the brain.

Our body's natural painkillers work at these same three links in the pain circuit. A soldier charged with adrenalin in battle may suffer grievous injury while unaware of the wound because the cerebral cortex ignores the pain signals while dealing with a highly emotional and life-threatening situation. In natural childbirth, a woman's body releases small proteins called endorphins that dampen the transmission of pain signals as they enter her spinal cord.

Hormones, emotional states and numerous other factors can also dramatically alter a person's perception of pain by modulating the transmission of messages along pain pathways. In addition, many biological processes and substances that alter the ebb and flow of molecules through ion channels in individual nerve cells all contribute to regulating the sensitivity of nerves themselves. When an injury occurs, these factors can ease controls on neuronal firing, thereby facilitating the neurons' job of transmitting pain signals.

That uninhibited state, however, can last too long, leaving DRG cells hypersensitized and causing them to fire pain messages without an external stimulus. This situation is the primary cause of neuropathic pain. The increased neural sensitivity can also cause abnormal feelings of tingling, burning, tickling and numbness (paresthesia) or, as in Helen's experience of the shower of daggers, can amplify light touch or temperature sensations to painful levels (allodynia).

Efforts to understand how neurons in the pain circuitry become hypersensitive after injury have, not surprisingly, long focused on what goes wrong in neurons—work that has yielded some clues but not a complete picture. My own research and that of many colleagues have demonstrated, for instance, that the very act of firing impulses to send pain signals alters the activity of genes inside pain neurons. Some genes regulated by neuronal firing encode the ion channels and other substances that heighten the cells' sensitivity. The intense activation of DRG cells when tissue is injured can thus cause the kinds of sensitizing changes in those neurons that might result in neuropathic pain later on. Our studies and the work of other laboratories also reveal, however, that neurons are not the only cells responding to painful injury and releasing the substances that promote neural sensitivity.

Glia far outnumber neurons in the spinal cord and brain. They do not fire electrical impulses, as neurons do, but they have some interesting and important properties that influence neuronal firing. Glia maintain the chemical environment surrounding neurons: beyond delivering the energy that sustains the nerve cells, they sop up the neurotransmitters that neurons release when they fire an impulse to a neighboring neuron. Sometimes glia even dispense neurotransmitters to augment or modulate the transmission of neuronal signals. When neurons are injured, glia release growth factors that promote neural survival and healing, and they release substances that call on cells in the immune system to fight infection and initiate healing. And yet recent research is revealing that these activities on the part of glia, to nurture neurons and facilitate their activities, can also prolong the state of neural sensitization.

Glia Become Suspect

For more than a century scientists have known that glia respond to injury. In Germany in 1894 Franz Nissl noticed that after a nerve is damaged, glial cells at the spots where nerve fibers connect in the spinal cord or brain change dramatically. Microglia become more abundant, and a larger type, called astrocytes because of their star-shaped cell bodies, becomes much beefier, plumped up with thick bundles of filamentous fibers that fortify its cellular skeleton.

These glial responses were commonly understood to promote nerve repair after injury, but how they did so was unclear. Furthermore, if an injury–such as a twisted ankle–is inflicted far from the spinal pain circuitry, the astrocytes in the spine must be responding not to direct injury but rather to changes in signaling at the relay point between DRG and spinal neurons. This observation implied that astrocytes and microglia were monitoring the physiological properties of pain neurons.

Over the past two decades glia have been shown to possess many mechanisms for detecting electrical activity in neurons, including channels for sensing potassium and other ions released by neurons firing electrical impulses and surface receptors for sensing the same neurotransmitters that neurons use to communicate across synapses. Glutamate, ATP and nitric oxide are among the significant neurotransmitters released by neurons that are detected by glia, but many others exist. This array of sensors allows glia to survey electrical activity in neuronal circuits throughout the body and brain and to respond to changing physiological conditions [see "The Other Half of the Brain," by R. Douglas Fields; *Scientific American*, April 2004].

Once scientists recognized the breadth of glial responses to neural activity, attention returned to the support cells' suspicious behavior at pain-relay points. If glia were monitoring neural pain transmissions, were they affecting them, too? Exactly 100 years after Nissl's observation of glia responding to nerve injury, a simple experiment first tested the hypothesis that glia might participate in the development of chronic pain. In 1994 Stephen T. Meller and his colleagues at the University of Iowa injected rats with a toxin that selectively kills astrocytes, then assessed whether the animals' sensitivity to painful stimulation was reduced. It was not, showing that astrocytes have no obvious role in the transmission of acute pain.

Next the scientists treated rats with a nerve-fiber irritant that caused the animals to gradually develop chronic pain, much as

Helen experienced long after the car accident irritated the nerves in her ankle. Animals injected with the astrocyte poison developed dramatically less chronic pain, revealing that astrocytes were in some way responsible for the onset of chronic pain after nerve injury. Subsequent research has revealed how.

Glia release many types of molecules that can increase the sensitivity of DRG and spinal cord neurons relaying pain signals to the brain, including growth factors and some of the same neurotransmitters that neurons themselves produce. Scientists have come to realize that glia interpret rapid neural firing and the neural changes it induces as a sign of distress in the neurons. In response, glia release the sensitizing molecules to ease the stress on the neurons by facilitating their signaling and to begin their healing.

Another vital class of molecules that glia generate in response to neuronal damage or distress are cytokines, which is shorthand for "cytokinetic," meaning cell movement. Cytokines act as powerful chemical beacons that cells in the immune system follow to reach the site of an injury. Consider the immense needle-in-the-haystack problem a cell in your immune system faces in finding a tiny splinter embedded in your fingertip. Potent cytokines released from cells damaged by the splinter beckon immune system cells from the blood and lymph to rush to the fingertip to fight infection and initiate repair. They also induce changes in the tissue and local blood vessels that ease the work of immune cells and promote healing but that result in redness and swelling. The collective effects of cytokine signaling are called inflammation.

A splinter demonstrates how effective cytokines are in targeting immune cells to a wound, but even more impressive is how painful a tiny splinter can be—the pain is far out of proportion to the minuscule tissue damage suffered. Soon even the area surrounding the splinter becomes swollen and painfully sensitive, although these neighboring skin cells were unharmed. The pain surrounding an injury is caused by another action of inflammatory cytokines: they greatly amplify the sensitivity of pain fibers. Supersensitizing pain sensors near an injury is the body's way of making us leave the site alone so that it can heal.

Neurons, as a rule, are not the source of cytokines in the nervous system–glia are. And just as cytokines can make the nerve endings surrounding a splinter in your fingertip hypersensitive, the cytokines released by glia in the spinal cord in response to intensive pain signaling can spread to surrounding nerve fibers and make them hypersensitive as well. A cycle may begin of oversensitized neurons firing wildly, which sends glia into a reactive state, in which they pour out more sensitizing factors and cytokines in an attempt to relieve the neurons' distress but end up instead prolonging it. When that occurs, pain can originate within the spinal cord from nerve fibers that are not directly injured.

The initial responses of glia to an injury are beneficial for healing, but if they are too intense or continue too long, unstoppable chronic pain is the result. Several research groups have documented the feedback loops that can cause glia to prolong their release of the sensitizing factors and inflammatory signaling that leads to neuropathic pain, and many are experimenting with ways to reverse those processes. This work has even led to ways of making the narcotics used in treating acute pain more effective.

Stopping Pain at Its Source

In the past, all treatments for chronic pain have been directed toward dampening the activity of neurons, but the pain cannot abate if glia continue to incite the nerve cells. Insights into how glia can fall into their vicious nerve-sensitizing cycle are leading to new approaches to targeting dysfunctional glia in the hope of stopping a fundamental source of neuropathic pain. Experimental efforts to treat neuropathic pain by modulating glia are therefore focusing on quieting glia themselves, blocking inflammatory trigger molecules and signals and delivering anti-inflammatory signals.

In animal experiments, for instance, Joyce A. DeLeo and her colleagues at Dartmouth Medical School have shown that a chemical called propentofylline suppresses astrocyte activation and thereby chronic pain. The antibiotic minocycline prevents both neurons and glia from making inflammatory cytokines and nitric oxide, as well as reducing the migration of microglia toward injury sites, suggesting the drug could prevent glial hyperactivation.

A related approach centers on Toll-like receptors (TLRs), surface proteins on glial cells that recognize certain indicators of cells in distress and prod glia to begin emitting cytokines. Linda R. Watkins of the University of Colorado at Boulder and her colleagues have shown in animals that using an experimental compound to block a particular TLR subtype, TLR-4, on glial cells in the spinal cord reversed neuropathic pain that stemmed from damage to the sciatic nerve. Interestingly, naloxone–a drug used to blunt the effects of opiates in addiction treatment, also blocks glial responses to TLR-4 activation. Watkins has demonstrated in rats that naloxone can reverse fully developed neuropathic pain.

Another existing drug, indeed an ancient pain-relieving substance that can work when many others fail, is marijuana, which has been legalized for medicinal use in some states. Substances in the marijuana plant mimic natural compounds in the brain called cannabinoids, which activate certain receptors on neurons and regulate neural signal transmission.

Two types of cannabinoid receptor occur in the brain and nervous system, however: CB1 and CB2. They have different functions. Activating the CB2 receptor brings pain relief, whereas activating CB1 receptors induces the psychoactive effects of marijuana. Remarkably, the CB2 receptor that relieves pain does not appear on pain neurons; it is on glia. When cannabinoids bind to microglial CB2 receptors, the cells reduce their inflammatory signaling. Recent studies have found that as chronic pain develops, the number of CB2 receptors on microglia increase, a sign that the cells are valiantly trying to capture more cannabinoids in their vicinity to provide analgesic relief. Now pharmaceutical companies are vigorously pursuing drugs that can be used to control pain by acting on glial CB2 receptors without making people high.

Blocking inflammatory cytokines with existing anti-inflammatory medicines, such as anakinra (Kineret) and etanercept (Enbrel), has also reduced neuropathic pain in animal models. In addition to stemming inflammatory signals, several groups have demonstrated that adding anti-inflammatory cytokines, such as interleukin-10 and IL-2, can subdue neuropathic pain in animals. Two existing drugs, pentoxyfilline and AV411, both inhibit inflammation by stimulating cells to produce IL-10. Moreover, assorted research groups have reversed neuropathic pain for up to four weeks by delivering the genes that give rise to IL-10 and IL-2 into the muscles or the spine of animals.

A few of these drugs have entered human trials for pain, including AV411, which is already used as an anti-inflammatory treatment for stroke in Japan. A trial in Australia showed that pain patients voluntarily reduced their dosages of morphine while on the drug, a sign that AV411 was contributing to relieving their pain. But AV411 may be working by mechanisms that go beyond calming pain caused by inflammation, highlighting a surprising twist in the tale of glia and pain.

Restoring Balance

Morphine is among the most potent painkillers known, but doctors are wary of its devilish properties, to the extent that many will undertreat even patients with terminal cancer. Like heroin, opium and modern narcotics, such as OxyContin, morphine blunts pain by weakening communication among spinal cord neurons, thus diminishing the transmission of pain signals.

Unfortunately, the power of morphine and other narcotics to block pain quickly fades with repeated use, a property called tolerance. Stronger and more frequent doses are necessary to achieve the same effect. Patients with chronic pain can become addicts, compounding their misery with debilitating drug dependency. Doctors, fearing that they will be suspected of *dealing* rather than *prescribing* such large quantities of narcotics, are often forced to limit patients to dosages that are no longer effective in relieving their agony. Some patients resort to crime to obtain illegal prescriptions to ease their intolerable pain; a few turn to suicide to end their suffering. A new finding at the intersection of pain relief, glia and drug addiction is evidence that glia are responsible for creating tolerance to heroin and morphine.

Suspicions about glial involvement in narcotic tolerance first arose with the observation that just as when an addict quits heroin "cold turkey," patients dependent on narcotic painkillers who stop their medication suddenly suffer classic painful withdrawal symptoms. The patients (and heroin addicts) become hypersensitive to such an extreme that even normal sound and light become excruciatingly painful. The similarity of these symptoms to the hyperesthesia seen in neuropathic pain suggested the possibility of a common cause.

In 2001 Ping Song and Zhi-Qi Zhao of the Shanghai Institute of Physiology tested whether the development of tolerance to morphine involved glia. When the researchers gave rats repeated doses of morphine, they saw the number of reactive astrocytes in the spinal cord increase. The changes in glia caused by repeated morphine injection were identical to those seen in the spinal cord after an injury or when neuropathic pain develops. The scientists then eliminated astrocytes with the same poison that Meller used to dampen the development of chronic pain in rats. Morphine tolerance in these animals was sharply reduced, indicating that glia in some way contribute to it.

Many research groups have since tried blocking various signals between neurons and glia (for example, by inactivating specific cytokine receptors on glia) and testing whether morphine tolerance is affected. This research shows that blocking inflammatory signals to and from glia does nothing to alter normal acute pain sensations, but if the blockers are injected together with morphine, lower doses of morphine are required to achieve the same relief and the duration of pain relief is doubled. These findings strongly indicated that glia were counteracting the pain-relieving effect of morphine.

Glia's actions to undermine the potency of morphine are in keeping with the fundamental glial job of maintaining balanced activity in neural circuits. As narcotics blunt the sensitivity of pain circuits, glia respond by releasing neuroactive substances that increase neuronal excitability to restore the normal levels of activity in neural circuits. Over time glial influence ratchets up the sensitivity of pain neurons, and when the blunting effect on pain circuits provided by heroin or narcotic pain medications is suddenly removed by rapid withdrawal from the drug, neurons fire intensely, causing supersensitivity and painful withdrawal symptoms. In experimental animals painful withdrawal from morphine addiction can be reduced dramatically by drugs blocking glial responses.

Modulating the activity of glia, then, could prove to be a key not only to alleviating chronic pain but also to reducing the likelihood that people treated with narcotic painkillers will become addicted. What a boon glia-targeted drugs would be for those who have long sought to control two such major sources of human misery and tragedy. Yet the connections among neurons, pain and addiction eluded scientists in the past who ignored the vital partner of neurons–glia.

About the Author

R. Douglas Fields an adjunct professor in the University of Maryland, College Park's Neuroscience and Cognitive Science Program. He is the author of the award-winning books Electric Brain *and* The Other Brain.

MIND on Pain: The Psychology of Pain

By Howard L. Fields

Several years ago an elderly man came into the emergency room at Cook County Hospital in Chicago with a large, painful abscess (boil) on the back of his neck. When I told him he needed a minor procedure to lance the boil and drain it, he became ashen, asking, "Doc, is this going to hurt?" I told him that if at any time the treatment hurt too much, he could tell me to stop—and I would. I opened the boil with a very sharp scalpel. He did not make a sound for some time. "When are you going to start?" he finally asked. "It's done," I said. "How did you do that?" he replied. "I didn't feel anything."

Most people think of pain as resulting from physical injury or disease, but psychological factors play a huge role in pain perception. In the case of my elderly patient, my reassurance that the treatment would not significantly worsen his pain—because he could stop me if it did—produced an analgesic effect. In addition, reducing the man's fear enabled him to look forward to pain relief instead, and that positive expectation also eased his pain.

The importance of mind-set to pain perception should come as no surprise. Pain is a warning sign of injury, but for such a sign to be useful, pain must influence human behavior in a way that increases survival. Thus, pain must be intimately tied to brain functions that govern behavior and decision making, including expectation, attention and learning. By way of these links, a painful blister on your foot can motivate you to stop walking or to protect the area with moleskin. It may also teach you to shop for more comfortable shoes or wear thicker socks in the future.

The interaction between the pain message and the brain centers that mediate motivation and learning accounts for the powerful effect of a person's state of mind on the severity of pain he or she experiences with any injury. It explains the placebo effect: the expectation that a sugar pill will relieve pain reduces the extent of the agony even though the pill has no pharmacological effect. Conversely, if you are convinced that an injection, say, will be very painful, you are likely to unwittingly amplify the sting. Mood also interacts with agony. Depressed people, for example, may feel more pain as a result of their sour state of mind. In fact, worsening of a long-standing pain problem, such as headache, often is the first sign of depression or at least the complaint that first brings a depressed patient to the attention of a physician.

Recent investigations are unraveling the mystery of how and when factors such as expectation of reward or punishment, fear, stress and mood alter perceived pain intensity and affect our daily decisions. Some of these psychological factors also influence the risk of developing a chronic pain condition. The research not only reveals just how far pain reaches into our psyches but also may lead to better ways of controlling pain and hastening recovery from painful injuries.

Mind over Matter

In the classic view of pain perception, a stimulus to the body excites pain-sensitive sensory neurons in the body's periphery; these neurons then transmit information in the form of electrical signals that eventually activate parts of the brain that enable us to perceive pain [see "When Pain Lingers," by Frank Porreca and Theodore Price. But for decades doctors have noted that a person's mental state can also dramatically affect pain perception.

For example, Harvard University anesthesiologist Henry K. Beecher noted in an article published in 1956 that soldiers who had been wounded in battle complained of much less pain than did patients with similar injuries in a civilian hospital. Beecher reasoned that in the context of having survived a battle and heading for home, an injury has a different meaning than it does for people hurt in the course of ordinary life. In the war scenario, a wound has honorable connotations, and such a positive spin on pain can lessen the sensation, Beecher speculated. Doctors have also long known about the analgesic powers of traumatic stress and of dummy pills that patients believe to be painkillers.

How could cognitive and emotional influences affect how much agony we feel? Over the past few decades researchers have uncovered a circuit in the brain and spinal cord that functions as a kind of volume control for pain, adjusting the amount a person perceives depending on the circumstances. In the early 1970s scientists at the University of California, Los Angeles, discovered that excitation of a small area in the midbrain of the rat produced profound pain relief. When they sent electricity through small wires implanted into that region of the brain, the rodent would no longer respond to intense, tissue-damaging stimuli that otherwise would make it squeak and flee. Later in the decade scientists showed that patients with severe chronic pain obtain significant, though temporary, relief from electrical stimulation of the same midbrain site, the periaqueductal gray.

Since then, researchers have mapped other parts of the body's pain-control circuit. It stretches from the brain's cerebral cortex in the frontal lobes through underlying brain structures, including the periaqueductal gray, to the spinal cord, where pain-sensitive nerve fibers connect to neurons that transmit pain signals from the rest of the body. Neurons in this pathway synthesize peptides known as endorphins that have pharmacological properties identical to the powerful opioid morphine. Endorphins, the body's natural painkillers, and opioids (which also include opium and heroin) act at the same receptors, called mu opioid receptors, along this pain modulatory pathway to produce their analgesic effects.

Great Expectations

Neuroscientists are finding that cognitive influences on pain operate through this modulatory pathway. The circuit is the conduit for a variety of expectation effects, including the prospect of pain relief from a placebo pill. In 2004, for example, neuroscientist Tor D. Wager, now at Columbia University, and his colleagues found that a placebo produced increased activity in this pain-control circuit. Endorphins seem to be important in transmitting the pain-suppressing signal: my colleagues and I found that blocking mu opioid receptors with the drug naloxone erases the placebo effect in patients experiencing pain from a recent surgery. [For more on placebos, see "Cure in the Mind," by Maj-Britt Niemi; *Scientific American Mind*, February/March 2009.]

Recent data from my laboratory implicate the same circuit in other forms of expectation while underscoring their power over pain. In a study published in 2006 my research team showed volunteers color cues generated on a computer monitor just before exposing them to a painful stimulus through a metal probe taped to their hand. The words "low temperature" against a blue background were followed by mildly painful heat, and the words "high temperature" against a red background by more intense heat. Afterward subjects were placed in a magnetic resonance imaging scanner and randomly shown the red-high and blue-low cues beginning just before the mild or intense painful stimuli were applied.

We found that the blue-low temperature cue, which had previously preceded milder discomfort, reduced the reported pain to the intense stimulus. In contrast, the red-high temperature cue, which had been paired with greater pain, amplified the discomfort of the mild stimulus. When the red-high cue preceded the intense stimulus, the pain magnitude was greatest. The brain sites known to be part of the pain transmission system in the thalamus and cortex were fully activated only when both stimulus intensity and high pain cues were given together. Thus, the pain we experience is a synthesis of what happens in our body and what we expect, which depends on what we are told or have otherwise learned.

We isolated the brain regions involved in the expectation effect by subtracting activity in the brain areas that lit up when the stimulus was intense and a person anticipated more pain from those excited by the same painful peripheral stimulus given when a person expected less pain. The net result was activation in cortical and brain stem regions that we now know are involved in the control of pain.

In addition to predictions about the pain itself, the expectation of a reward—say, from food or drugs—can profoundly affect pain intensity. In a classic 1984 experiment pharmacologists J. Dum and Albert Herz of the Max Planck Institute for Psychiatry in Munich fed rats every day while the rodents were standing on a metal plate, which was at room temperature. Some of the rats ate regular rat chow, whereas the others feasted on chocolate-covered biscuits. After two weeks, the researchers placed the rats on the plate, which they then gradually heated to a painful temperature. The rats that had previously consumed their regular chow responded to the pain after four seconds; the rats that expected to receive chocolate endured the heat for twice as long. When the rats received a drug that prevents endorphins from relieving pain, however, the animals would no longer wait twice as long for their chocolate treat. Thus, the anticipation of the food reward had served as an analgesic, effectively raising the rats' tolerance for pain.

Food, sex and other natural enticements—and even the mere anticipation of such pleasures—activate the brain's reward circuitry in both rodents and humans. In doing so, they can also produce pain relief. The effects of opioid drugs further suggest that reward and pain relief have a partially shared neural basis. After all, the most powerful of these drugs, such as morphine and oxycodone (OxyContin, a prescription painkiller that has been widely abused), can relieve severe pain but also unleash a "high"—leading to their addictive potential.

Painful Choices

Pain and reward interact at mu opioid receptors. Mice engineered to lack a functioning mu receptor experience neither pain relief nor reward from morphine. In addition, rats given naloxone (which blocks opioid receptors) no longer experience pain suppression when they are expecting a food reward such as chocolate. Thus, when a person anticipates a reward such as a delicious dinner, the body releases endorphins, activating the mu receptors along the descending pain-control pathway and controlling pain signals as they enter the central nervous system.

A brain region called the nucleus accumbens plays a critical role in both signaling reward and controlling pain. Inactivating this region, which contains mu receptors, prevents animals from experiencing pleasure from either recreational drugs or natural rewards such as food and sex. What is more, injecting rewarding substances into this region can suppress pain responses.

The ability of an imminent prize to suppress pain can influence decision making in situations in which reward seeking and escape from pain are in conflict. An athlete, for example, may face a choice between giving in to physical discomfort and enduring it in hopes of winning a race or a game. A person with a painful blister on his foot might have to choose between resting the injury and going out for pizza and a movie. Such decisions depend on a cost-benefit analysis inside the brain. How painful is the injury, and how much do you expect to enjoy the victory, movie or pizza? These expectations influence your decisions, in part through the pain-control circuit.

If you are a highly motivated athlete or you expect the pizza or movie to be extremely good, your expectation will–through the release of endorphins and their stimulation of mu receptors–not only enhance the predicted enjoyment of the victory, food or film but also suppress pain. The overall effect biases you toward tolerating the pain to reach your goal or reward. In addition, you will actually *feel* less pain as you compete or head to town.

Similarly, rats that anticipate chocolate subconsciously "decide" to bear the pain of a hot plate to get the chocolate, both because they expect it to taste delicious and because that expectation alone reduces their pain. Such a resolution of pain-reward conflicts may have survival value. Animals often must endure pain to fight off a competitor for food or for a desirable mate.

The analgesic properties of anticipated rewards are consistent with the placebo effect. If relief of pain is rewarding, then a placebo pill is a sign of a forthcoming reward, leading to pain suppression. Thus, the expectation of relief becomes a self-fulfilling prophesy.

Conversely, predicting pain has the opposite effect, amplifying activity in the pain transmission pathway and leading to greater pain perception.

Positive expectations for healing from painful injuries can lead to faster actual recovery from those wounds. In 2009 epidemiologist J. David Cassidy of the University of Toronto and his colleagues reported that among 2,335 Saskatchewan residents who endured traffic-related whiplash injuries, which are a major source of neck pain, those who expected to get well enough to return to their regular job reported recovering 42 percent faster than did those who were less positive. Previous studies have also shown that expectations for recuperating are consistently associated with going back to work among patients who have lower back pain, suggesting that a person's outlook on the future can strongly influence how much pain impinges on his or her life.

Skirting Danger

In addition to expectations of recovery or reward, a sense of danger can squelch pain. Researchers, including psychologists Fred. J. Helmstetter of the University of Wisconsin–Milwaukee and Michael S. Fanselow of U.C.L.A., have shown that rats do not respond to painful stimuli in the presence of a predator or when the rats are in an environment that provokes fear because, say, they had previously experienced a painful stimulus in it. Naloxone blocks this analgesic effect of fear in rats, indicating that the presence of imminent danger suppresses the experience of pain through release of an endogenous opioid.

People will often feel no pain during or immediately after severe trauma—say, a traffic accident or incident on a battlefield or during an athletic contest. Situations that produce acute tissue injury may signify an ongoing hazard and thus unleash fear or acute stress in humans and animals. The resulting suppression of pain may enable a person or animal to get to safety before being hobbled by agony.

Although acute stress can suppress pain, if stress persists and becomes chronic, pain usually intensifies. A bad mood may also increase pain. People who suffer from depression, for instance, may be more vulnerable to or less tolerant of pain. A 2007 study of 131,500 Canadians showed that among chronic pain patients, 11.3 percent had major depressive disorder as compared with just 5.3 percent of individuals who did not experience chronic pain. Being in pain may be depressing, and depression itself is also thought to affect pain perception. Neurochemical changes associated with depression–such as the depletion of the neurotransmitters serotonin and norepinephrine–may reduce normal inhibition or increase facilitation within the descending pain pathway.

In addition, catastrophizing, or interpreting pain as unbearable and likely to worsen, tends to increase the experience of pain. Patients who score high on catastrophizing on a standard questionnaire tend to experience more severe pain after surgery and show more sensitivity to experimentally induced pain than do those who score low on the questionnaire. Catastrophizing may worsen pain by making a person concentrate on it and attach additional emotion to it. In a study published in 2004 rheumatologist Daniel J. Clauw of the University of Michigan at Ann Arbor and his colleagues tested 29 fibromyalgia patients for their tendency to catastrophize and then measured their brain responses to blunt pressure on a thumbnail. They linked pain catastrophizing to increased activity in brain areas related to the anticipation of pain, attention to pain and emotional aspects of pain perception.

Psychological distress of various forms raises a person's risk of developing a pain syndrome. In a study published in 2007 neurobiologist William Maixner of the University of North Carolina at Chapel Hill and his colleagues tracked 244 initially pain-free women for up to three years to see who developed temporomandibular joint disorder, a condition characterized by persistent jaw pain, to determine the traits that foretell its development. They linked being depressed and feeling stressed, for example, with a twofold to threefold rise in the chance of getting the disorder. In earlier work, scientists at the University of Washington tied somatization—a tendency to report numerous symptoms in excess of that expected from a physical injury—with more than a doubling of the incidence of the disorder and less improvement after five years.

Parting with Pain

Research into the psychology of pain may lead to new ways of helping people overcome or cope with pain caused by injury, medical treatment or disease, whether minor or significant. Already, increased knowledge of the brain circuits that mediate the interaction of reward and pain relief is beginning to provide clues for strategies to dissociate the addictive potential of drugs from their pain-relieving power. The findings may lead to effective painkillers that are significantly less addictive than opiates.

In addition, understanding the powerful effects of mood, expectation and other psychological factors on pain is important for helping friends, patients or loved ones deal with their pain. Telling people in pain about individuals who have done well can often ease their distress and discomfort, whereas informing them of others who have had serious illnesses with similar symptoms will very likely worsen their suffering.

Doctors should be on the lookout for mood-related factors such as depression or chronic stress that might be abetting a patient's pain. They also need to carefully query patients about, or otherwise assess, their expectations regarding their discomfort. If a patient is overly pessimistic, a physician can reassure him or her by providing more accurate information, as I did with the man I treated for the abscess. Ultimately, the new understanding of the effects of mind-set on pain promises to revolutionize our approach to pain treatment.

The Battle over Pain in the Brain

By Diana Kwon

Pain is an unpleasant but necessary sensation. The few people born without the ability to feel it must approach day-to-day tasks with extra caution. Without the ability to sense the effects of a broken bone or burned skin, it's difficult to avoid harm. On the other hand, too much pain can be debilitating. Individuals with chronic pain often experience a host of additional negative effects on mental and physical health. Despite recent advances in uncovering the underlying mechanisms of pain perception in the brain, scientists are still debating the questions of where and how pain is processed.

Over the years neuroscientists have identified the "pain matrix," a set of brain areas including the anterior cingulate cortex, thalamus and insula that consistently respond to painful stimuli. Some researchers have since applied this concept to conclude that that rejection hurts because social pain and physical pain share similar mechanisms in the brain. Others have suggested that brain imaging could be an objective measure of pain for diagnosis and drug development, and even as evidence in court.

In recent years, however, a number of studies have cast doubt on the idea that these brain areas are specifically coding for pain. In the most recent study, published this week in *JAMA Neurology*, neuroscientists at the University of Reading and University College London scanned the brains of two individuals born without the ability to feel pain and four healthy volunteers while they received painful "pinprick" stimuli. The scientists found similar patterns of activity in the brain areas widely associated with pain in both groups, providing evidence that the pain matrix may be responding to other senses.

"If this was the only evidence that we had so far, I would be a bit more cautious in the interpretation," says André Mouraux, a neuroscientist at Université Catholique de Louvain in Belgium who was not involved in the study. However, this is not the first piece of evidence that these areas are not specific to pain. For example, in 2011 Mouraux and his colleagues discovered similar activations in the brains of healthy individuals to both painful and non-painful stimuli. "Altogether, the story becomes convincing," Mouraux says. Because the pain-related regions are involved in so many other cognitive processes, most researchers are adopting the view that the pain matrix is more generally responsible for processing attention-grabbing stimuli.

According to the study's authors, the idea of a pain matrix is still pervasive and drives many incorrect scientific conclusions. "It is very tempting to put someone in the scanner, give a stimulus causing pain and record a brain response that–often, but not always–correlates with the intensity of the pain perceived, and conclude that the response reflects pain," says Giandomenico Iannetti, a neuroscientist at University College London.

Finding Pain in the Brain

Pain's locus in the brain is hotly contested subject. Recently, a number of high-profile papers reporting brain areas specific to pain have come under fire. For example, in March 2015 a group at Oxford University published a study in *Nature Neuroscience* claiming that the dorsal posterior insula was the "ouch center" of the brain. The study received widespread criticism from the pain research community, including an article by several influential scientists rebutting the claims. Researchers have since found that this area is actually responsive to both painful and non-painful stimuli.

Then in December a group of neuroscientists at the University of California published a paper in *PNAS* claiming that another area, the dorsal anterior cingulate cortex, was selective for pain. This too led to a critical reaction paper, this time in the same journal that published the original study.

The biggest issue with these studies–and many neuroimaging studies–are the limitations of reverse inference, where researchers use types of brain activity, sometimes referred to as "blobs" for the shapes they form on fMRI scans, to deduce that a specific cognitive event like processing pain is occurring. While this is technically not impossible to do, especially with new techniques that apply machine learning, "blobology" is a very tricky business.

Take the dorsal anterior cingulate cortex, for example. Neuroscientists have associated it with a variety of functions in addition to pain, including attention, working memory and conflict monitoring, meaning that when this region lights up in a scanner, any number of these processes could be occurring.

Some researchers are not too impressed with the recent *JAMA Neurology* results, either. According to Tor Wager, a neuroscientist at the University of Colorado, "They're not isolating the pain-related activity in controls and so they don't have a basis for quantifying the difference." What they should have done, he says, is measure the change in brain activity as the painful stimulus increased in the group that could feel pain, then compare this to the change in activity in the pain-free individuals while they received the same stimulus.

Wager believes that while areas in the pain matrix may not be specific to pain, certain patterns of activity in this network are. His group found evidence of this in a 2013 study in which they reported distinct patterns of activity for physical and social pain within similar brain regions. "I believe, until proven otherwise, that the pain network is largely encapsulated within the pain matrix," Wager says. "But it doesn't mean that measuring the blobs is sufficient."

Beyond the Blobs

Although the search for pain markers in the brain may sound like battle of wits between academics, there are high stakes to this endeavor. The costs of chronic pain—in terms of medical expenses and lost productivity as well as suffering and opioid addiction—are tremendous. To measure pain, clinicians currently rely largely on patients to report how they feel. These ratings are highly subjective, which can be an issue for drug development—for example, when researchers try to rule out placebo effects. Having a neuroimaging technique that could reliably detect pain signals could be a hugely beneficial tool for diagnosis and drug development.

There are limitations to keep in mind, however. "The most dangerous utility is [using neuroimaging] to rule out that somebody is in pain," says Tim Salomons, a neuroscientist at the University of Reading and head author of the current study. Rather than identifying whether someone is experiencing pain, neuroimaging will more likely be helpful in providing information about how much pain a person is feeling or how effective a drug is in mitigating pain. "People are suffering and we actually could do something about that–but we [first] have to understand the science better," Wager says.

About the Author

Diana Kwon is a freelance journalist who covers health and the life sciences. She is based in Berlin.

Is Pain a Construct of the Mind?

By Stephen L. Macknik & Susana Martinez-Conde

> We are more often frightened than hurt; and we suffer more from imagination than from reality.
>
> –Lucius Annaeus Seneca

Dennis Rogers is an unassuming guy. He's on the short side. And though muscular, he doesn't come across as the kind of towering Venice Beach, muscle-bound Arnold that you might expect from someone billed as the World's Strongest Man. Rather he has the kind of avuncular intensity you find in a great automobile mechanic–a mechanic who happens to be able to lift an engine with one hand while using the fingertips of the other hand to wrench the spark plugs out. Like it's nothing. Rogers, who has been known to keep two U.S. Air Force fighter planes from blasting away in opposite directions by holding them back with his bare hands, performed at the most recent Gathering for Gardner–a conference that celebrates the interests of one of *Scientific American*'s greatest columnists, the late mathemagician Martin Gardner. We asked Rogers about the source of his incredible powers after the show, and we were surprised to learn that he did not know. Bill Amonette of the University of Houston–Clear Lake found that Rogers could recruit an abnormally high number of muscle fibers. But was this ability because of a freak genetic mutation? Another possibility, which Rogers thinks is more likely, is the way he processes pain when he strains those muscles.

What if, instead of superpowered muscles, Rogers has a normal–though extremely well exercised–body, and his abilities arise because he can withstand more pain than most mere mortals? He claims that he does feel pain and is actually scared of dentists. In fact, during one stunt in which he held back four souped-up Harley motorbikes with straps, he bit down so hard he split a tooth from top to bottom. Rather than taking his chances at the dentist, he reached into his mouth, clamped his viselike fingertips onto the broken tooth, and extracted it, root and all.

Rogers reasons that, unlike in the dentist's office—where he has no control over the pain that is inflicted on him—he has direct executive control over pain that he inflicts on himself. "I know it's coming, I have an idea of what to expect and I can decide to ignore it," he says. Confronted with severe pain, most people fear that they will damage their body permanently if they persist, so they stop well before they are in real danger, Rogers explains. He does not stop and only rarely gets seriously hurt.

Maybe Rogers's muscle cells are normal, and he experiences pain as most of us do but chooses to disregard it when he feels in command. If so, he has become strong not because he was born on a planet with a red sun like Superman or was trained in the Danger Room of Charles Xavier's School for Gifted Youngsters like an X-Man but because, when he has a job to do, he *doesn't care* that it hurts.

An illusion is a perception that does not match the physical reality. Is pain, then, as with illusions, a mind construct that some people can decide to turn off? As you will see in the studies that follow, pain varies as a function of mood, attentiveness and circumstances, lending support to the theory that pain is an emotion. These studies show that empathy also extends to pain, just as it does to other emotions, even when the victims are fake strangers. And the research indicates that people can experience pain for the wrong reasons or fail to experience it when it would be very reasonable to do so. Moreover, when pain is disconnected from the physical reality, it is an illusion, too.

About the Authors

Stephen L. Macknik is a professor of opthalmology, neurology, and physiology and pharmacology at SUNY Downstate Medical Center in Brooklyn, N.Y. Along with Susana Martinez-Conde and Sandra Blakeslee, he is author of the Prisma

Prize-winning Sleights of Mind. *Their forthcoming book,* Champions of Illusion, *will be published by Scientific American/Farrar, Straus and Giroux.*

Susana Martinez-Conde is a professor of ophthalmology, neurology, and physiology and pharmacology at SUNY Downstate Health Sciences University in Brooklyn, N.Y. She is author of the Prisma Prize–winning Sleights of Mind, *along with Stephen Macknik and Sandra Blakeslee, and of* Champions of Illusion, *along with Stephen Macknik.*

Neuroscientists Identify a Brain Signature of Pain

By Michele Solis

Like truth and beauty, pain is subjective and hard to pin down. What hurts one moment might not register the next, and our moods and thoughts color the experience of pain. According to a report in April in the *New England Journal of Medicine*, however, researchers may one day be able to measure the experience of pain by scanning the brain—a much needed improvement over the subjective ratings of between one and 10 that patients are currently asked to give.

Led by neuroscientist Tor Wager of the University of Colorado at Boulder, researchers used functional MRI on healthy participants who were given heated touches to their arm, some pleasantly warm, others painfully hot. During the painful touches, a scattered group of brain regions consistently turned on. Although these regions have been previously associated with pain, the new study detected a striking and consistent jump in their activity when people reported pain, with much greater accuracy than previous studies had attained. This neural signature appeared in 93 percent of subjects reporting to feel painful heat, ramping up as pain intensity increased and receding after participants took a painkiller.

The researchers determined that the brain activity specifically marked physical pain rather than a generally unpleasant experience, because it did not emerge in people shown a picture of a lover who had recently dumped them. Although physical pain and emotional pain involve some of the same regions, the study showed that fine-grained differences in activation separate the two conditions.

A brain-based marker of pain might someday help doctors assist people who have difficulties communicating, such as the very young or victims of stroke. Yet Wager does not see this neural signature as a pain "lie detector." "There are many psychological and physiological ingredients that go into a person's report of pain, and we've discovered just one ingredient here," he says. Many states of brain activity very likely give rise to pain, Wager adds, "pain is not just one thing."

Pain's Many Idiosyncrasies

Even as researchers make strides in understanding and treating pain, new discoveries raise many more questions. These recent findings reveal the deep connections between pain and many essential physical and mental processes.

- Patients with chronic back pain tend to be impaired at emotional learning but have increased sensitivity to taste.
- Chronic pain shrinks the brain, up to 11 percent in some cases.
- Those with chronic pain can learn to control their perception of pain by imagining pleasant scenarios or believing a particular stimulus to be harmless.
- Memory of a pain can cause that pain to persist for life, even after the initial injury has healed.
- Chronic pain sufferers can learn to associate a place with their pain. Returning to this space can reinforce the negative association.

MIND on Pain: When Pain Lingers

By Frank Porreca & Theodore Price

Imagine you are a doctor treating a patient who has been in nearly constant pain for four years, ever since the day he sprained his ankle stepping off a curb. Physical therapy only briefly dulled the agony. Painkillers were not much better, and the most effective drugs made your patient exhausted and constipated. He is now depressed, sleeping poorly and having difficulty concentrating. As you talk with him, you realize that his thinking also seems impaired. Your exam confirms that the original injury has healed. Only pain and its consequences remain–and your options for helping this man are running out.

This scenario plays out every day in doctors' offices around the world. Fifteen to 20 percent of adults worldwide suffer from persistent, or chronic, pain. Half the primary care patients who develop a chronic pain condition fail to recover within a year, according to surveys conducted by the World Health Organization. Common causes of such unrelenting discomfort include physical trauma, arthritis, cancer, and metabolic diseases such as diabetes that can damage nerves. In many cases, however, the pain's origins are mysterious.

Indeed, despite decades of intense research into the biology of pain and how pain is perceived, many mysteries still surround chronic pain and its treatment. No one knows for sure why some injuries, even minor ones, result in persistent pain or why it occurs in some people but not in others. Nevertheless, researchers are pinpointing telltale changes in the neurons that underlie persistent pain. In particular, they have documented abnormal excitability among neurons at every level of the body's pain network. For instance, in the spinal cord, some cells aberrantly amplify pain signals after undergoing a type of molecular "learning" that is similar to what happens in the brain during the formation of long-term memories.

Chronic pain is more emotionally fraught than acute pain—which comes on quickly but lasts a relatively short time. Changes in brain regions governing feelings and complex thoughts in chronic pain states may help explain some of the unwanted emotional and cognitive problems, from depression to attention deficits, that can sometimes emerge after years of suffering. Researchers have even uncovered signs that chronic pain might be a type of neurodegenerative disease, affecting parts of the brain that deal with attention, memory and decision making. A firmer understanding of these processes could lead to new treatments that would alleviate the relentless chronic pain experienced by millions of people worldwide.

Disease of Discomfort

We sense pain using specialized sensory neurons called nociceptors; these cells extend to most of the body, their fibers running alongside other sensory neurons in large bundles that make up peripheral nerves. Nociceptors normally respond selectively to strong stimuli, such as pressure, heat or cold. They then send their messages to neurons in the spinal cord, which, in turn, relay neuronal indications of potential or real tissue damage to the brain centers where pain perception occurs. Activation of this pain pathway is critical for reflexive and coordinated protective responses to escape something that could damage the body, such as a stinging insect or a hot stove. Detecting circumstances in which we might experience harm is a vital protective function of our nervous system.

But the protective pain we experience as a result of daily living is quite different from that which leads patients to seek medical attention. Instead of becoming active only in the presence of strong and potentially damaging stimuli, the pain transmission pathway can become pathologically revved up in reaction to movement of joints, light touch or other actions that are normally innocuous—a phenomenon termed allodynia. In some sufferers, donning clothes, taking a shower or going for a walk on a breezy day is excruciating because the fabric, water or wind on their skin abnormally stimulates pain pathways.

In other cases, pain can occur spontaneously, without any obvious cause. Patients who have endured nerve damage as a result of diabetes, for example, may feel intense burning pain while doing nothing more than sitting quietly in a chair.

Unlike ordinary pain messages, spontaneous pain and pain produced by mild stimulation do not signal impending damage to tissues and do not provide a survival advantage. Pain produced under these conditions reflects pathological changes in pain pathways and represents a disease in and of itself.

Too Much Excitement

In the early 1980s researchers began to learn the sources of such pathological pain. Studies in rats by neuroscientist Clifford Woolf of University College London and Harvard University and his colleagues revealed, for example, that following an injury to a rat's paw, neuronal signals from nociceptors near the skin to neurons in the spinal cord became amplified, much like turning up the volume on an iPod. These altered neurons unleash exaggerated reactions to tissue-damaging input; in addition, they become more easily excited, responding to stimuli that are ordinarily too mild or weak to produce a reaction.

Hormones or inflammatory molecules that the body produces in response to injury may sensitize nociceptors, making them more impulsive, a change that could instigate the development of chronic pain and abnormal sensitivity to mild stimuli. (Such molecules also account for the aches a person may feel during normal movement a day after lifting weights, an activity that can lead to mild muscle damage.) Chronic pain conditions often begin when a peripheral nerve is injured, making that nerve—a bundle of fibers of which some are nociceptors—and neighboring ones more excitable. Hyperexcitability within the uninjured nerves that intermingle with the wounded nerve is probably paramount for the persistence of pain after the original injury is gone because many of the damaged nerves degenerate.

In addition to becoming more excitable, injured neurons may sometimes start signaling spontaneously. Injuries to peripheral nerves from trauma, diseases such as diabetes and cancer, drug treatments or excessive use of recreational drugs such as alcohol can spark such relentless electrical discharge, or ectopic activity, in the damaged nerves. These nerves then provide persistent input to the rest of the pain transmission pathway, a process that is believed to drive spontaneous pain. Often the recalcitrant signaling that underlies the pain remains long after an injury has healed.

In recent years researchers have revealed a molecular basis for this low-level ectopic activity. Voltage-gated sodium channels—proteins that conduct sodium ions into a cell in response to voltage changes—on the membranes of these neurons are essential for their ability to transmit electrical messages; their abundance and activity—how often they open and shut, for example—play an important role in how sensitive or excitable a neuron is. The latest data indicate that in chronic pain states these channels cluster where they count most, at the endings of the neurons near the skin and all along the nerve, most likely making the neurons more responsive to input.

For example, in a 2003 study one of us (Porreca) and his colleagues used fluorescent molecules to visualize a sodium channel called Na_v1.8 in the peripheral nerve cells of rats after a type of nerve injury that leads to chronic pain. We saw that the nerve membrane undergoes a "remodeling" so that the Na_v1.8 channels accumulate near the injury. This study suggests that injury prompts the nerve cells to ship lots of these proteins from their neuronal cell bodies near the spinal cord outward to the nerve terminal. This redistribution appears to be critical to the experience of neuropathic pain, because blocking the cells from producing this sodium channel made the rats' pain disappear, as evidenced by a return to their normal behavior. Neuroscientists have also discovered support for a similar transport of sodium channels in human tissues from studies on patients who have nerve injuries that produce persistent pain.

Other researchers have been homing in on the underpinnings of chronic pain in the dorsal horn of the spinal cord, where the peripheral pain fibers end. In 1999 neuroscientist Patrick W. Mantyh, then at the University of Minnesota, and his colleagues found that a subset of these dorsal horn neurons—just 1 to 3 percent of cells in this region—of the spinal cord are major culprits in chronic pain. Using a Trojan horse strategy, they chemically coupled a toxin to a neurotransmitter, a neural signaling substance, so that when the neurotransmitter bound to its receptor on another cell, the receptor-transmitter complex served as a chemical "scalpel," deleting (killing) the recipient cell. Without these dorsal horn neurons, rats failed to show signs of chronic pain after local inflammation or nerve injury—symptoms that plagued rats that still had these neurons. The elimination of this neuronal subset did not affect ordinary pain perception, however, implicating these cells primarily in pathological discomfort.

But what happens in these spinal cord neurons when pain becomes chronic? Recent data hint that they undergo a process called long-term potentiation (LTP), a long-lasting improvement in communication between two neurons that also underlies the formation of certain types of memories in the brain. Although LTP in the brain generally requires high-frequency input, 100 hertz or above, in a 2006 study neurophysiologist Jürgen Sandkühler of the Medical University of Vienna and his colleagues demonstrated that low-frequency stimulation from injured peripheral nerves in rats can lead to LTP in some dorsal horn neurons. In LTP, input from one neuron leads to a heightened response in the recipient cell, an effect that should enable spinal cord cells to amplify incoming pain signals. And just as LTP represents a molecular mechanism of memory storage in brain cells, it may underlie the ability of spinal cord neurons to sustain a state of chronic pain.

Nerve circuits that arise in the brain and lead down to the spinal cord can also profoundly influence the incoming pain signals and the resulting experience of pain. In this circuit, cells in the periaqueductal gray area of the midbrain receive input from the various regions of the brain's outer layer (the cortex) as well as from interior sections, such as the amygdala and the hypothalamus. This midbrain region then relays information to the rostral ventromedial medulla (RVM) in the brain stem, the lower part of the brain adjoining the spinal cord. Activation of this circuit mediates the powerful suppression of pain that occurs during trauma, intense stress or excitement.

This same circuit, and in particular the RVM, also plays a major role when pain from an acute injury persists. Work from our laboratories has shown that when nerves are injured in rodents, a specific set of cells in the RVM sends out a signal that amplifies, rather than diminishing, incoming pain signals and sets the stage for chronic pain. In 2001, for example, a team led by Porreca used the toxin-based Trojan horse strategy to selectively snip out these RVM neurons in rats. Without these cells, the rats still developed pathological pain in their hind paw after a nerve injury, but that pain was short-lived, suggesting the RVM harbors a critical "switch" for the maintenance of chronic pain.

In an important 2008 study neuroscientist Irene Tracey of the University of Oxford and her colleagues found that neural activity in this brain stem region in human volunteers paralleled the duration of painful symptoms (induced by exposure to the hot pepper compound capsaicin) that were similar to those of chronic pain patients. Current evidence suggests that ectopic input from injured nerves may alter these RVM cells so that their messages to the spinal cord facilitate, instead of inhibiting, incoming pain signals.

Painful Feelings

In addition to operating the pain-control circuit, pain-processing regions of the brain interpret input from the spinal cord and from other brain regions to create an overall impression of the discomfort. This interpretation depends on the setting and on a person's past experience, attentiveness and mood, among other psychological factors [see "The Psychology of Pain."] To that end, pain not only stimulates sensory areas of the brain but also powerfully activates brain areas involved in emotion, such as the anterior cingulate cortex (ACC), a region governing emotional aspects of pain, and the amygdala, which mediates fear and other feelings. These areas—which are part of a so-called pain axis in the brain—can become hyperactive in chronic pain conditions and may, in turn, play a significant role in enhanced responses to stimulation in these patients.

Various known triggers of chronic pain seem to alter the ACC in particular. Peripheral nerve injury and chronic inflammation precipitate neural restructuring in the ACC. In addition, psychological factors such as mood, expectation and hypnotic suggestion can modulate pain responses in the ACC, according to human imaging studies [see "The Truth and the Hype of Hypnosis," by Michael R. Nash and Grant Benham; *Scientific American Mind*, June 2005]. Thus, the ACC may integrate sensory input with emotional state and may partially underpin some of the "affective" disturbances associated with chronic pain, such as depression, sleep disorders and pain catastrophizing, a condition in which patients expect and fear that pain will be intense and unmanageable. (Neuroscientists have shown that pain catastrophizing specifically engages the ACC.) The involvement of the ACC and the pain axis in general might also help explain the common occurrence of pain in patients with conditions such as depression and post-traumatic stress disorder.

A hyperactive pain axis not only increases pain intensity but also augments the aversive qualities of the experience. Chronic pain may thus reflect a switch from a bottom-up condition in which painful sensory information dominates to a top-down state in which emotional and cognitive assessments control pain behavior.

Certain cognitive deficits may also result from the toll chronic pain takes on patients. In 2004 neuroscientist A. Vania Apkarian of Northwestern University's Feinberg School of Medicine and his colleagues demonstrated that individuals with chronic back pain or complex regional pain syndrome, a debilitating condition that can develop after trauma, showed a decreased ability to accurately assess risk and reward when making decisions. All the patients took part in the Iowa Gambling Task, a card game in which players choose between "bad" decks of cards that yield high immediate gain but substantial future losses and "good" decks that produce lower immediate gain but minimal losses later. Pain-free participants chose cards from the good decks—the most profitable strategy—more frequently than the pain patients did. The patients also tended to be fickle, frequently switching between decks, suggesting that the unpleasant emotions that accompany a state of persistent agony may interfere with judgments in other situations, such as weighing options in a gambling game.

In recent work presented at international pain meetings, neuroscientists Volker Neugebauer of the University of Texas Medical Branch and Vasco Galhardo of the University of Porto in Portugal showed that arthritic rats display a similar impairment. Given a choice between a "high-risk" food-dispensing lever that yields three food pellets in three out of 10 visits and a "low-risk" lever promising one pellet eight times out of 10, arthritic rats over time developed a preference for the high-risk lever (risking going hungry in seven of 10 visits), whereas normal rats more consistently picked the low-risk lever (missing only two snacks in 10). In this study the researchers associated a change in the brain with the inappropriate risk assessment: alterations in chemical signaling within neural circuits connecting the amygdala to the prefrontal cortex—a region governing higher cognitive functions, including attention, decision making and working memory—of the arthritic rats.

Previous work by Neugebauer and his colleagues suggests that chronic experimental pain in rats can lead to amplification of neural signals coming into the so-called nociceptive amygdala, a part of the amygdala governing pain. This augmented input then magnifies the messages—which are inhibitory in nature—that the nociceptive amygdala sends to the prefrontal cortex. The increased inhibition of the prefrontal cortex may impair an animal's (or human's) ability to accurately assess the risks of options when making important decisions.

More obvious brain changes may underlie other types of cognitive decline, among them muddled thinking and difficulty concentrating, in chronic pain patients. In 2004 Apkarian and his colleagues reported a shrinking of the prefrontal cortex in patients with very long-lasting back pain. The decreased brain volume was proportional to the duration of the pain in these patients but roughly equivalent to that seen in 10 to 20 years of aging. Since then, other research teams have revealed preliminary evidence of possible atrophy in the brains of some patients afflicted with other persistent pain conditions. These results hint that pain might actually be a neurodegenerative disease leading to remodeling of the prefrontal cortex and possibly other cognitive regions of the brain.

No one knows for sure how chronic pain could lead to neurodegeneration, but the increased neuronal excitability that we now know characterizes chronic pain may provide a clue. Such excitability often leads to excessive release of the neurotransmitter glutamate, and glutamate is known to be toxic to neurons in large quantities. At this point, however, the glutamate explanation is purely speculative, and researchers are actively investigating various possible molecular causes of this neurodegeneration.

Calming Nerves

The recent insights into the mystery of why pain becomes chronic may point to new therapies. Medical researchers are attempting to block amplification of neuronal signals at every stage of the body's pain network. A few current and emerging medicines are geared toward countering abnormal activation of nociceptors. Some of these therapeutics act as "sponges" to absorb inflammatory proteins or nerve growth factors that are thought to boost the excitability of these pain-transmitting neurons. Other compounds that target neuronal hyperexcitability include sodium channel blockers and inhibitors of enzymes such as nitric oxide synthase that yield active neurotransmitters.

In the future, new analgesics might target the small subset of cells in the dorsal horn of the spinal cord that Mantyh, now at the University of Arizona, and his team tied to chronic pain or analogous cells in the RVM. A better understanding of the role of the ACC in chronic pain conditions might lead to novel therapeutic strategies that ameliorate pain, along with its psychological consequences. Ideally, these antiamplification therapies will not only ease patients' suffering but also prevent structural brain changes and possibly neurodegeneration that accompany extreme forms of chronic pain. That is, the best treatments would not just reduce symptoms but also reverse the disease process.

Drug treatments might make up just a part of the eventual strategy for ending intractable pain. Advanced diagnostic techniques might help determine the underlying cause of persistent pain. Some researchers are trying to identify "biomarkers," or molecular signs, of chronic pain that they could find in a blood or tissue sample, enabling early detection–and treatment–of abnormal changes in the nervous system that signal chronic pain. This technique could also point to the therapies most likely to work in an individual.

For patients who have a long-standing problem, doctors may want to prescribe behavioral techniques to address any emotional and cognitive fallout from the pain. Patients might be advised, for example, to supplement their medication with mind-preserving strategies, including intellectual challenges such as puzzle solving and physical exercise. Such a multipronged attack on relentless pain and its consequences should ultimately offer greater hope for the afflicted.

Subliminal Messages Influence Our Experience of Pain

By Simon Makin

Most people associate the term "subliminal conditioning" with dystopian sci-fi tales, but a recent study has used the technique to alter responses to pain. The findings suggest that information that does not register consciously teaches our brain more than scientists previously suspected. The results also offer a novel way to think about the placebo effect.

Our perception of pain can depend on expectations, which explains placebo pain relief–and placebo's evil twin, the nocebo effect (if we think something will really hurt, it can hurt more than it should). Researchers have studied these expectation effects using conditioning techniques: they train people to associate specific stimuli, such as certain images, with different levels of pain. The subjects' perception of pain can then be reduced or increased by seeing the images during something painful.

Most researchers assumed these pain-modifying effects required conscious expectations, but the new study, from a team at Harvard Medical School and the Karolinska Institute in Stockholm, led by Karin Jensen, shows that even subliminal input can modify pain–a more cognitively complex process than most that have previously been discovered to be susceptible to subliminal effects.

The scientists conditioned 47 people to associate two faces with either high or low pain levels from heat applied to their forearm. Some participants saw the faces normally, whereas others were exposed subliminally–the images were flashed so briefly, the participants were not aware of seeing them, as verified by recognition tests. The researchers then applied a temperature halfway between the high and low levels, alongside either one of the conditioned faces or a previously unseen face. Participants rated how painful the new temperature was.

The faces previously linked with high or low pain increased and reduced pain ratings, respectively, relative to the new face. The finding held whether the participant had seen the faces normally or learned the association subliminally.

"Our results demonstrate that pain responses are shaped by expectations we may not be aware of," Jensen says. If this applies to the placebo effect generally, one way it could have a beneficial effect is if our mind makes implicit connections between medical paraphernalia and getting better. Hospital settings or a doctor's behavior might then facilitate a placebolike effect. The finding also adds to the growing body of research showing that information that never reaches our conscious awareness can nonetheless influence our later behavior.

Abou the Author

Simon Makin is a freelance science journalist based in the U.K. His work has appeared in New Scientist, *the* Economist, Scientific American *and* Nature, *among others. He covers the life sciences and specializes in neuroscience, psychology and mental health. Follow Makin on X (formerly Twitter) @SimonMakin*

Does Financial Insecurity Lead to More Physical Pain?

By Daisy Grewal

The Great Recession led to a dramatic increase in the number of Americans living with day-to-day economic insecurity. According to the Survey of Economic Risk Perception and Insecurity, 93 percent of U.S. households experienced a decline in their wealth between 2008 and 2009. A more recent study by the Federal Reserve suggests that financial insecurity is fairly common. For example, 47 percent of survey respondents said they would have difficulty covering an emergency expense of $400.

Growing financial insecurity has been accompanied by another trend: an increased number of Americans who report living with physical pain. The National Survey on Drug Use and Health reported that dependence on painkillers increased by 50% between 2006 and 2012. In 2008, the estimated economic cost of pain exceeded the combined cost of cancer, heart disease, and diabetes.

A research team led by public policy Professor Eileen Chou at the University of Virginia hypothesized that the confluence of these two trends – greater economic uncertainty and more physical pain – may not be entirely coincidental. Chou and her colleagues recently published a paper in *Psychological Science* summarizing six studies that demonstrate a direct link between financial insecurity and the experience of physical pain.

The first study looked at a diverse sample of 33,720 American households and found that households in which one or more of the primary adults are unemployed spend more money on painkillers. This finding held steady even after the researchers statistically controlled for other factors that could be linked to the purchase of pain medication, such as the number of people living in the household, total household income, and consumption of cold and flu medications. While suggestive, these findings don't prove that economic insecurity causes more pain. To test this hypothesis, the researchers designed experiments where they manipulated people's feelings of economic insecurity.

In one study, they recruited online participants and randomly assigned half of them to write about a time in their lives when they felt uncertain about their economic future, for example, due to job instability. The rest of the participants were asked to write about a time when they felt secure about their economic future. Afterwards, all participants completed a short survey asking the amount of pain they were currently experiencing in their head, chest, or stomach. Chou and her colleagues found that participants who had written about a time when they felt insecure about their finances reported almost twice as much pain as those who wrote about a time when they felt financially secure. It's important to point out that the researchers manipulated people's subjective feelings of financial insecurity rather than their actual financial situations. Therefore, how people feel about their financial situations, regardless of their actual economic well-being, may have important consequences for physical health.

Why would feelings of financial insecurity lead people to report higher levels of physical pain? Several previous studies have shown that psychological pain and physical pain share similar brain pathways. This may explain why taking painkillers has been shown to reduce both physical and emotional pain. In addition, Chou and her colleagues hypothesized that financial insecurity may cause people to feel less control over their lives, which in turn, leads to heightened feelings of pain. Their assumption is based on past research showing that people who feel less control over their lives are at higher risk for physical health problems.

To test their hypothesis, the researchers conducted a study where they manipulated people's feelings of control. Using online participants, they randomly assigned half of the people in their study to write about a time in their lives when felt a lack of control. The remaining participants were assigned to write about an incident in their life when they felt like they were in complete control of what has happening to them. After the writing exercise, participants indicated how much pain they were experiencing at that very moment. Those who had written about a time when they felt a lack of control reported more than twice the amount of physical pain than those who wrote about a time when they felt complete control. Feelings of control may at least partly explain how economic insecurity leads to more physical pain.

Although suggestive, the research presented by Chou and her colleagues is only a very early step. Most likely the factors at play are complex. For example, anxiety and depression are also associated with greater reports of physical pain. While both of these conditions stem from a lack of perceived control, they are also frequently accompanied by low self-esteem.

Nevertheless, Chou's research provides an important perspective on how economic insecurity directly impacts people's physical well-being. Understanding this connection may point towards solutions that could help people get back on their feet – both financially and physically. After all, physical pain can severely limit or even preclude someone's ability to hold down a steady job, thereby leading to more financial insecurity. Figuring out how to intervene, perhaps by finding ways to restore people's feelings of control over their lives, might lessen physical pain as well as provide the best chance of helping people regain their financial footing.

About the Author

Daisy Grewal holds a B.A. in psychology from the University of California, Los Angeles, and a Ph.D. in social psychology from Yale University. She is a research scientist on the people analytics team at Intuit in Mountain View, Calif.

Section 2: The Unique Experience of Pain

MIND on Pain: Why People Experience Pain Differently

By Ingrid Wickelgren

One day as a child Billy Smith (not his real name), a resident of Newfoundland, could not take off his shoe. No amount of twisting or tugging would loosen its grip on his foot. The reason for his struggle eventually surfaced: a nail had pierced the sole and entered Smith's flesh, tightly binding the two. Removing the nail freed the foot, but solving that problem only underscored a bigger one: Smith had not noticed.

Smith is among a tiny cluster of people, fewer than 30 in the world, who harbor a genetic quirk that renders them incapable of perceiving pain. "These humans are completely healthy, of normal intelligence, but don't know what pain is," says clinical geneticist C. Geoffrey Woods, who studied a group of such patients from northern Pakistan. They can sense touch, heat, vibration and their body's position in space. Yet for them, root canals are painless, as are falls, fires and whacks on the head with a baseball bat. One woman with so-called congenital indifference to pain (CIP) delivered a baby without discomfort.

"The children have lots of bruises, cuts and scalds from exploring like kids do, but with no pain to restrict their activities," Woods says. One Pakistani boy entertained others by sticking knives in his arms and leaping out of trees. Before Woods could see the child, he died jumping off a roof. The kids who survive are often deformed and disabled by self-mutilation or broken bones that they failed to notice or refused to rest. When Smith was three, he fractured a bone in his foot but kept walking on it as if nothing had happened.

Although such cases are exceptional, doctors and scientists have known for decades, if not centuries, that human beings at large differ greatly in how sensitive they are to pain. Much of the variation is apparently random. But gender matters. Women tend to hurt more than men do. Ethnicity can also interface with ache; some ethnic groups are more tolerant of discomfort than others are.

In the past few years, as technological advances have eased the deciphering of the human genome, researchers have begun unearthing the genetic roots of these differences. They are also pinpointing social, cultural and psychological factors that play parts in pain sensitivity. The multitude of influences on pain refutes the conventional conception of this sensation as an index of tissue damage. Thus, assessing patients' vulnerability to anguish may be essential to accurately judging the severity of their condition. It is also critical to deciding how to treat their pain. Revealing the molecular causes of individual variation in pain perception is already helping to unravel the biology of agony and providing targets for novel pain medications.

Spectrum of Suffering

Physicians have long noticed wide disparities in the pain tolerance of the people they treat. Among patients with the same condition, pain ratings typically range from "no pain" to "the worst pain imaginable." And although some disorders are more painful than others, the variation in distress among individuals with the same physical malady is far greater than the difference in the discomfort people feel, on average, from one condition to the next. "Two soldiers may be shot in the same nerve," says Stephen G. Waxman, a neurologist at Yale University and the Veterans Administration Connecticut Health Care Center. "One has sensory loss but is otherwise okay; the other has intractable burning pain."

Objective indicators of physical harm often correspond poorly to perceived pain. In one study the amount of inflammation in rheumatoid arthritis patients did not parallel the degree of suffering they reported. In people with osteoarthritis, the tissue damage shown on an x-ray often bears little relationship to the amount of discomfort a patient feels. Even when a scientist carefully controls the intensity of a painful procedure–say, a cold bath or compression of a limb—people significantly differ in how much they say it stings. (On the other hand, an individual's evaluations of agony are surprisingly consistent. If you ask someone to hold an object that becomes increasingly hot to tell you when the pain starts, that moment will be the same—within 0.2 degree Celsius—every time you repeat the procedure, even a few years later.)

What a person says about pain does jibe with changes in the brain if not the body. In a 2003 investigation neurobiologist Robert C. Coghill of the Wake Forest University School of Medicine and his colleagues asked 17 adults to evaluate the pain they felt from a hot metal device touching their lower leg. At the same time, the researchers scanned the volunteers' brains using functional magnetic resonance imaging. Pain-related regions of the brain were more active in the individuals who judged the twinge as more intense than they were in less sensitive subjects, Coghill and his colleagues found.

Verbal pain ratings also predict a person's vulnerability to chronic pain. In 2007 neurobiologist William Maixner of the University of North Carolina at Chapel Hill and his colleagues tested healthy female volunteers for pain sensitivity and psychological functioning. The researchers then tracked them for three years to determine who would acquire temporomandibular joint disorder (TMJD), which causes persistent discomfort in the joints on either side of the ear where the upper and lower jaw meet. Sixteen of 243 women came down with classic TMJD, and the disorder was three times more likely if a woman was very sensitive to pain than if she was relatively insensitive, Maixner says. His team has also associated elevated sensitivity to painful stimuli with other persistent pain syndromes such as fibromyalgia.

Gender Bias

For a decade or longer, researchers have known that women are at greater risk than men for a number of chronic pain conditions, including rheumatoid arthritis, lupus and fibromyalgia. Women are also more sensitive to noxious stimuli: in laboratory experiments the average woman exhibits a lower pain threshold (the point at which she first feels pain) and less pain tolerance (the degree or duration of pain she can stand) than the average man.

Sex hormones may contribute to this gender difference. Estrogen, for example, can often increase pain, in part by acting at receptors that sit on pain nerves. During her menstrual cycle, a woman perceives more pain after ovulation when progesterone—and to a lesser extent, estrogen—levels are high, consistent with the idea that female hormones intensify pain. In addition, hormone replacement therapy increases pain sensitivity in women, whereas drugs that stymie estrogen's actions provide long-term pain relief in certain situations. (In other circumstances, such as pregnancy, high levels of female hormones are accompanied by diminished pain perception; scientists do not fully understand why.)

Male and female brains seem to register discomfort differently. In 1999 Coghill's team reported that women perceived the same painful stimulus as more intense than men did and showed more activity in brain regions involved in processing pain. This excess excitement may stem in part from a weaker network for blocking pain. In 2002 psychiatrist Jon-Kar Zubieta, now at the University of Maryland, and his colleagues gave 14 men and 14 women an excruciating injection of saline into their cheeks while scanning their brains, focusing on parts of a "descending" pain-thwarting pathway in which endorphins, the body's natural painkillers, bind to mu opioid receptors to squelch the pain signal after acute injury [see "The Psychology of Pain," by Howard L. Fields]. In the males this pain-curbing network was flooded with more endorphins and activity at mu opioid receptors than it was in females—a sign of a more powerful pain-control system.

Other evidence points to weaker pain inhibition in women. Intense or long-lasting pain applied to one part of the body, say, an arm, can suppress pain at another site, such as a tooth. The initial pain is thought to invoke the body's descending pain suppression system. In 2003 neuroscientist Donald D. Price of the University of Florida College of Dentistry and his colleagues showed that this phenomenon was less pronounced in women: in men, dunking one hand into a painfully hot bath diminished the discomfort of a scorching object touching the other hand, but the women felt no such relief.

Emotional and social factors may also contribute to women's enhanced pain sensitivity. For instance, women tend to engage in pain-related catastrophizing–that is, expecting that pain will be awful and unbearable–more than men do. On the other hand, men are typically less willing than women to admit to being in pain because men want to appear tough and strong.

But pain is not necessarily a sign of weakness. In fact, women's tendency toward discomfort might be adaptive. Women are generally more attuned to bodily sensations than men are and have a greater capacity to sense all environmental stimuli, such as light, noise and odor, which may improve their ability to detect threats. Some scientists argue that evolutionary pressures may have promoted such a trait in women to enable them to better protect their offspring.

Not only are women more prone to pain, so are certain ethnicities. African-Americans display greater sensitivity to painful stimuli in the laboratory and report more negative emotional responses to pain than Caucasians do.

Cultural, social and psychological factors probably contribute to this disparity. In a study published in 2007 clinical psychologist Roger B. Fillingim, also at the University of Florida College of Dentistry, and his colleagues demonstrated that a person's ethnic identity–that is, the degree to which a person relates to a minority group's ancestry, language, physiology and culture–strongly affects his or her pain sensitivity. The researchers tested 63 African-Americans, 61 Hispanics and 82 non-Hispanic whites for their susceptibility to pain from a hot object touching their arm, very cold water surrounding a hand, and constriction of blood flow to an arm. Each person also filled out a questionnaire called the Multigroup Ethnic Identity Measure (MEIM).

The researchers found that the range of temperatures and the time that a person was willing to endure pain were lower for members of the two minority groups than they were for whites. And for the African-Americans and Hispanics, but not the whites, the stronger a participant's ethnic identity as judged by the MEIM, the greater his or her sensitivity to any of the types of pain. "Within a minority group the greater your ethnic identity, the greater your pain sensitivity," Fillingim concludes. Cultural factors related to ethnic identity such as religion, education or social expressiveness might bestow specific meanings on pain or suggest coping strategies, he posits. Such shared beliefs and practices may not only influence people's outward expressions of pain; they may also sculpt the biological infrastructure that underlies the experience of pain.

Some of that physiology apparently differs between African-Americans and whites. In 2008 Fillingim and his colleagues tested the natural pain suppression elicited by a strong or prolonged sensation of pain in 29 African-Americans and 28 whites. They induced ischemic pain, depriving an arm muscle of oxygen, by squeezing the arm with a tourniquet; during that procedure, they electrically shocked each person's ankle. The researchers found that ischemic pain produced greater reductions in electrical pain ratings in whites than it did in African-Americans, who may have a weaker inhibitory pathway. "This suggests that African-Americans are less effective at controlling pain than whites," Fillingim says.

Spectacular Mutations

Of course, individuals within a gender or ethnic group also vary in their sensitivity. Genes account for 22 to 60 percent of the variance, according to studies comparing the correspondence in this trait between fraternal twins, who share about half of their genes, with that between identical twins, who have virtually the same DNA.

In rare cases, such as those with a congenital indifference to pain, a single gene has a huge effect. Smith and others like him have a mutation in a gene for a tiny molecular gate, or channel, that sits on the endings of nerves that sense pain. The channel ordinarily serves as an amplifier of neural signals and appears to be necessary for all types of pain perception. In patients with the mutation, the channel does not work, knocking out pain perception. "This spectacular observation seals the case, at least in the extreme, that genetics can have profound effects on sensitivity to pain," says Stanford University anesthesiologist David Clark.

Other mutations in the same channel protein make its gate flip open more readily and stay open too long, turning up the amplifier instead of knocking it out. This molecular mishap results in the flip side of Smith's perilous indifference to pain: an existence infused with agony. Patients experience mild warmth as searing or scalding heat. They liken slipping on socks to pouring hot lava on their feet, Waxman says. One teenager's pain gets so severe that he requires anesthesia in an intensive care unit [see "The Pain Gate," by David Dobbs; *Scientific American Mind*, April/May 2007].

Subtler genetic tuning of this channel could underlie more ordinary variation in pain sensitivity. Woods has unpublished data fingering a relatively uncommon change in a single base pair that makes the channel more responsive and its bearers feel a moderate amount of additional pain, about the level that could be countered by codeine.

Inherited Ache

Common variants of genes for other proteins, including enzymes, appear to underlie a hardiness to hurt, or the opposite. The enzyme catecholamine-O-methyltransferase (COMT) breaks down the stress hormones adrenaline and noradrenaline (also known as epinephrine and norepinephrine) as well as dopamine, a brain chemical involved in reward and mood. If this enzyme is scarce or not working properly, stress hormone and dopamine levels rise, and that chemical bounty apparently intensifies pain. Fibromyalgia patients and people with facial pain have higher levels of these chemicals. People who are disposed to pain such as females or chronic pain patients also often have relatively sluggish COMT.

Lethargic COMT can result from an alteration in the gene for the enzyme, leading to a threefold to fourfold reduction in its function. In a study published in 2003 Zubieta and his colleagues found that people who had at least one genetic blueprint for the less active enzyme were more sensitive than those with only active COMT to pain from intramuscular injections of saline, requiring less saline to reach the same level of agony.

In recent years Maixner, geneticist Luda Diatchenko, also at the University of North Carolina, and their colleagues linked two other versions of the same gene, along with the one Zubieta studied, with distinct levels of pain sensitivity—low, average and high—as well as with vulnerability to chronic pain. (Zubieta evaluated the "average" version, for the enzyme with lower activity.) The researchers analyzed the gene in 202 healthy women, whom they also tested for sensitivity to 16 types of painful stimuli and followed for three years to determine which ones developed TMJD. Compared with the other versions of the gene, the variant conferring low pain sensitivity gives rise to vastly greater quantities of COMT and lowers a woman's risk for TMJD more than twofold.

These COMT alternatives account for 11 percent of the variability in human pain perception, the largest contributor to pain sensitivity people have found so far, Diatchenko says. COMT type is a better predictor of the risk of developing a chronic pain condition than cholesterol level is for cardiovascular disease risk, Maixner adds.

The link between COMT and pain turns out to involve intermediaries called beta-adrenergic receptors that sit on pain-sensitive nerve endings. Adrenaline stimulates these receptors, whose activation (by drugs) can result in an agonizing arthritislike syndrome. Variation in the genes for these receptors, too, can shape pain perception. Maixner's group has nabbed one version of the gene for the beta-adrenergic 2 receptor, which is especially responsive to epinephrine and thereby sensitizes a person to pain.

Diversity in pain sensitivity may also arise from different forms of the mu opioid receptor, which also influence responses to opioid drugs. Opioids such as morphine and the body's endogenous painkillers exert their pain-suppressing effects by acting on this receptor. Responses of patients to opioid painkillers vary widely. The lowest effective dose may be five to 10 times higher for some patients than for others, and in 25 percent of patients morphine is ineffective or causes intolerable side effects.

In 2009 Diatchenko and her colleagues looked at the mu opioid receptor gene in 196 females who were also scored for their sensitivity to a battery of painful stimuli, including those that were hot, piercing and squeezing. After analyzing the gene at 25 places at which a chemical unit tends to vary between individuals—so-called single nucleotide polymorphisms (SNPs)—the researchers found one site associated with pain sensitivity. The rarer version of this SNP, carried by 6 percent of the population, seemed to make a person pain-prone and relatively unresponsive to opioid medication; its more common counterpart, on the other hand, conferred high pain tolerance and a good morphine response.

Other genetic differences may also impinge on a person's response to opiates. Certain human enzymes metabolize medications, and the results of their actions may be required to make the drugs effective and nontoxic. For example, a liver enzyme known as CYP2D6 converts codeine into morphine, the substance that relieves pain. In 7 to 10 percent of Caucasians, however, codeine does not work, because these individuals' CYP2D6 enzyme cannot accomplish the conversion. On the other hand, 1 to 7 percent of whites have multiple copies of the same gene. These individuals break down codeine extremely quickly, making even low doses of the drug potentially toxic. In one 62-year-old man with this gene duplication, a small dose of codeine nearly killed him, according to a report from Geneva University Hospital in Switzerland.

The genes nabbed so far probably represent just a tiny fraction of the body's Lilliputian conspirators in creating or modulating pain. "At the end of the day, there will be scores to hundreds of genes related to explaining individual differences in pain," predicts behavioral geneticist Jeffrey S. Mogil of McGill University.

Tailoring Treatments

Careful assessment of a patient's pain sensitivity could be invaluable for preventing and treating pain. Pain-sensitive patients are, for example, likely to experience a lot of discomfort after surgery and thus may require a higher-than-average dose of a painkiller. "Even in people who had identical surgeries, there can easily be a severalfold difference in the amount of pain reliever a person will need during recovery," Clark says.

An awareness of such differences may also help doctors better assess the severity of a person's illness. Low pain sensitivity might, for example, mask the true seriousness of a patient's condition. In contrast, an unusually strong reaction to a painful event might exaggerate the degree of physical injury it caused.

Evaluating the pain tolerance of healthy patients may help doctors identify who is most vulnerable to developing persistent pain syndromes and thus who might want to forgo elective surgeries or take preventive analgesics after accidents or trauma. Genetic tests may further clarify a patient's risk. "Combining a couple of these genes together could give us good predictive value for who is likely to develop several persistent pain syndromes," Maixner says.

Testing people for variations in the mu opioid receptor or metabolic enzymes might further reveal who will respond well to opioids and at what dose and who might benefit from alternative therapies. Responses to future generations of analgesics might also depend on a patient's genetic makeup. "It's critical to understand the impact of genetics on the treatment of a patient," Clark says.

Unearthing genes involved in pain perception, or lack thereof, can also pave the way toward new therapies. Pharmaceutical and biotech scientists, including those at Xenon Pharmaceuticals in British Columbia, are trying to discover and build molecules that silence the sodium channel that is out of order in congenital insensitivity to pain. "It looks very hopeful that people will have a new generation of painkillers" that target this molecule, Woods says.

Blocking beta-adrenergic receptors may help treat pain conditions stemming from either low COMT activity or high adrenaline levels, or both. In 2007 Maixner's team found that inhibiting beta-adrenergic receptors in rats that had poor COMT function prevented the animals from showing signs of heightened pain sensitivity. In a study published in 2009 Maixner, along with neuroscientist Kathleen C. Light of the University of Utah and colleagues, found that propranolol, which treats high blood pressure by blocking beta-adrenergic receptors, decreased pain in 10 fibromyalgia and 10 TMJD patients as compared with a dummy medication.

Even without genetic tests, doctors may one day base their prognosis and treatments on a person's gender, ethnicity and individual psychology. Some genetic differences seem to be more common among certain genders or races, in accordance with group differences in pain sensitivity. Unpublished work by Fillingim and his colleagues, for example, indicates that a form of the mu opioid receptor associated with stronger natural pain control is far less frequent in African-Americans than it is in whites.

The science of pain peculiarities also helps all of us to gain a better appreciation of pain in those around us. We cannot assume that another person's pain is inconsequential even if the injury looks unimpressive or would not be painful to us. Indeed, the pain perceived, almost by definition, exaggerates or minimizes the damage inflicted, given that pain stems from biological quirks particular to the sensation itself, along with cultural, social and psychological influences.

Of course, extreme cases of pain indifference put the survival value of our aches in stark relief. Despite the unpleasantness of pain and the commercial quest for ever more powerful analgesics, humanity cannot afford to wipe out pain the way it might strive to end cancer or heart disease. "We might joke that we wish we felt no pain, but that would be terrible–and is terrible for those who can't experience pain," Clark says. Aside from their physical injuries, people like Smith must endure a dollop of emotional isolation resulting from their inability to experience a virtually universal sensation. They keep quiet about this void. When they fall, they pretend that it hurts, because they want to be normal.

About the Author

Ingrid Wickelgren is a freelance science journalist based in New Jersey.

It's Time To Rethink the Origins of Pain

By Haider Warraich

Every person who has ever felt pain has their origin story, and I certainly have mine.

While performing a bench press more than a decade ago when I was in medical school, I heard a loud click and felt my whole body go limp, and the weights came crashing down. As pain gripped my entire body in a vise, I was rushed to emergency room where I got intravenous painkillers and was told the pain would eventually disappear.

But it didn't. And what I've learned about pain since has me seriously questioning how we diagnose and treat it.

I'm a doctor now, and in researching a book on pain, I've begun to understand that the reason the acute pain from my back injury turned into unrelenting chronic pain was likely in my brain. What determines the transformation of transient aches into ceaseless agony is not only explained by anatomy but often by psychology. Our perception of pain—and our fear of it—can play a huge role in clinical outcomes. However, far from minimizing people's experiences, this understanding is opening the door to treatments that might finally (and durably) help the millions living in unending torment.

I'm now a doctor, and our traditional approach in medicine has been to find mechanical and anatomic explanations for chronic pain; I was told from the MRI of my back that I had abnormalities so profound for a young person (I was just 20 years old), I had become the dreaded "interesting case" discussed at the radiology department's weekly conference. My bones were degenerating, and I had multiple damaged discs in my spine. Without any visible scars or deformities that were outwardly apparent, the MRI scans were the only evidence for what turned my acute injury into never-ending torment.

Chronic pain is usually defined as pain that affects someone frequently for three months or more, and mine exceeded that defined period by many years. I was reluctant to take painkillers and focused all of my energies on physical therapy. My pain has improved over time, but my origin story–the injury and the resulting abnormalities that showed up on the MRI–has had little to do with the pain I felt years afterward. "The classic idea is that if the injury is bad enough, it will stay on," Vania Apkarian, one of the world's leading pain researchers, told me. "But the injury itself has no value."

MRIs, while reliable indicators of injury, are not reliable indicators of pain. A review of studies that involved scanning images from about 3,000 people with no symptoms of back pain found that in 20-year-olds without any back pain, 37 percent had disc degeneration, and 30 percent had disc bulges. These abnormalities should cause pain, but for these people, they didn't. These abnormalities that show up in medical scans only increase with age, as 96 percent of 80-year-olds had disk degeneration and 84 percent had bulges. Even in people whose backs hurt, MRI abnormalities have shown absolutely no correlation with their pain–in other words, an MRI doesn't help us figure out what hurts and what doesn't. These data upended my narrative.

This is a really big deal: millions of people in the U.S., alone get MRIs and CT scans for back pain, which is the most common cause of disability around the world. Most of these tests are inappropriate since guidelines now recommend against the routine use of imaging for people with back pain. Yet a recent study showed that only 5 percent of MRIs ordered by clinicians for back pain were appropriate, and of those who received MRIs, 65 percent received potentially harmful advice emanating from the scans–including calls for back surgery.

Spine surgery is one of the most commonly performed procedures in the United States and around the world, but it can have devastating effects: in one study of people who had chronic back pain, of the people who had spine fusion surgery, only 26 percent returned to work compared with 67 percent of people who didn't have surgery. The people who chose surgery were more likely to develop complications and permanent disability than the people who didn't. I could have been one of those people: when I took my MRI films to Ather Enam, a renowned surgeon, he told me that an operation might leave my back worse off. "I could do the surgery, but a spine that's been touched by a surgeon is never the same again," he said.

So if anatomy doesn't explain why pain turns chronic, what does? Turns out that at least part of the cause was in my head.

One of the major reasons why pain becomes immortal in our bodies is how we feel in our minds. People who fear being in pain or are anxious about it are up to twice as likely to develop chronic pain after undergoing an operation. A study from Finland published this April showed that the presence of psychological distress significantly affected the presence or absence of back pain in those with degenerated spines. In fact, one small study showed that past traumatic events such as being robbed, bullied or sexually assaulted, were the strongest predictors of back pain turning chronic in the study's 84 participants; even the early fear of pain becoming permanent becomes a self-fulfilling prophecy.

Although in clinical medicine and societal discourse, mind and body, sensation and emotion, biology and psychology, are often considered as distinct, human nature begs to differ. In fact, these dichotomies collapse most dramatically when it comes to pain. As acute pain turns chronic, Apkarian's research shows it activates parts of the brain more responsible for emotions than physical sensations.

A recent clinical trial published in the *Journal of the American Medical Association: Psychiatry* indicates the power of therapies that target how we feel about hurting. In the study, led by Yoni Ashar and Tor Wager, the scientist who discovered the neurologic signature of pain in the brain, patients with chronic low back either received usual care mostly involving pain medications and physical therapy, were told they were getting a placebo (which can be quite effective for back pain) or received pain reprocessing therapy, which teaches people that the brain actively constructs chronic pain in the absence of an active injury and that simply reframing the threat pain represents can reduce or eliminate it. Such therapy defangs chronic pain of its sharpest weapon—fear. The results were quite remarkable: Of those people who received pain processing therapy twice-weekly for a month, 52 percent were pain-free at one year, compared with 27 percent of those receiving placebo and 16 percent receiving usual care. Patients also experienced improvements in disability, anger, sleep and depression.

Embracing the complexity of pain, especially chronic pain, can open the door to new and innovative ways to ensure that even if we hurt, we don't suffer. Therapies like pain reprocessing therapy embrace pain for what the science reveals it to be—as much an emotional and traumatic construct as a physical sensation. Such a holistic embrace of pain's nature, far from making us not take it seriously, should spur efforts even further to make sure everyone in agony receives kindness and respect, as well as access to more than pills and surgical procedures on their path to healing.

About the Author

Haider Warraich, a physician at Brigham and Women's Hospital, Harvard Medical School and the VA Boston Healthcare System, is author of The Song of Our Scars: The Untold Story of Pain *(Basic Books, 2022). Follow Warraich on Twitter @ haiderwarraich*

Section 3: Pain Disorders

Why Headaches Remain One of Medicine's Most Misunderstood Disorders

By Rachel Feltman, Fonda Mwangi, Alex Sugiura & Jeffery DelViscio

Rachel Feltman: For *Scientific American's Science Quickly*, I'm Rachel Feltman.

Headaches are incredibly common, but they've gotten surprisingly little attention from scientists.

Here to walk us through what we know—and don't know—about headache science is Tom Zeller, Jr. He's a former *New York Times* reporter and editor and the current editor in chief of *Undark*. He's also the author of a new book called *The Headache*.

Thanks so much for coming on to chat with us today.

Tom Zeller, Jr.: Oh, it's great to be here. Thanks for having me.

Feltman: So I would love to start with a little bit about what inspired you to write a book about headaches.

Zeller: Sure, well, you probably could guess that I have headaches myself. And not just the ordinary sort of headaches that we all get, but I have something called cluster headache, which is one of the three primary headache disorders—I mean, there are other primary headache disorders, but these are the three main ones: tension-type headache being the most common, migraine being probably the most familiar and most debilitating—and predominantly among women. Cluster headache is far more rare and more common among men, and that's what I have.

So, you know, it's an issue that I've sort of grappled with for most of my adult life. It's not something that I ever wrote about as a journalist, or thought that I ever would. But when I started thinking about a book I realized that I'd kind of been researching this topic for most of my life for other reasons, and so it seemed like a natural fit.

Feltman: And what is the research landscape like when it comes to these, you know, three major headache types?

Zeller: Yeah, it's surprisingly bleak. I mean, in the book I focus mostly on migraine because if there is any research being done, it tends to be on that. And to some extent I think it's fair to assume that what we learn about migraine will shed light on other headache disorders, too, because there's sure to be some underlying biology that they all share.

But in general the surprising thing to me that I discovered was how little we actually know about what's actually going on inside, like what bits of anatomy are being pulled into the choreography of a migraine attack, what bits of anatomy are more important than others.

And we know some. I mean, the research suggests–there are a lot of good imaging studies that show certain parts of the brain lighting up. There are more recent studies that indicate that certain neurochemicals are in abundant supply in the blood when someone is undergoing an attack. And we also know that the blood vessels may or may not play a role in all of this. But that's the extent of our knowledge of what's happening in migraine headache.

Feltman: Yeah, and how is it that we know so little when headaches are so ubiquitous?

Zeller: I think there's a lot going on. I think one of the most obvious things is that migraine mostly affects women, and I don't think I'm saying anything that you don't already know: that women's health in general has gotten short shrift over the decades. And so to the extent that women were more often presenting in clinicians' [offices] with migraine over the course of the 20th century, it was not taken very seriously ...

Feltman: Mm.

Zeller: And I think that that, in a lot of ways, it bled into decision-making at institutions like the [National Institutes of Health], which is the biggest funder of basic science in the U.S. So I think that's part of it.

I also think that there's something sort of cultural about the word "headache." I mean, we use this word as a metaphor for a mere annoyance: You know, "Doing your taxes is a headache." "Sitting in traffic is a headache." And it's unfortunate that we often have the same word to describe real neurobiological disorders. So that's at play, too.

And I think a third leg of it is the fact that we all get this thing called headache. If you don't have enough water, or you've skipped lunch, you have a little too much to drink the night before, you get a bit of a headache. So we all sort of think that we know what a headache is, and yet there is this sort of subset of people who have *headaches*, in a disorder sense ...

Feltman: Yeah.

Zeller: That are excruciating. And yet we use the same word to describe it. So I think all of those things sort of combined slowed the science on headache.

Feltman: Yeah, no, I think there's a real sort of definition problem. I, for years, thought I didn't get migraines but would kind of use the word for when I was feeling a particular kind of bad way. And then in the midst of having long COVID my migraines got more frequent and worse, and the increase in degree made me be like, "Oh, no, this is what people are talking about [laughs] when they say they have a migraine," which is just–it was so funny to me.

Zeller: Do you get the whole suite of symptoms? Like, you get the aura and all that, too, or just?

Feltman: It's really interesting, during the period where they got very bad and frequent I did have, like, the aura, the blurred vision, so that was really what made it like, "Oh, this kind of weird, bad feeling I sometimes get that comes with a headache ..."

Zeller: Yeah.

Feltman: "Is a migraine." And now it's much less common that I have this sort of whole suite, but yeah, they're wild, and it–you know, I have a friend who gets migraines that honestly present as kind of, like, strokelike ...

Zeller: Mm-hmm.

Feltman: Have, have, like, really intense–though brief and, you know, passing–neurological effects. And the fact that she can go to her neurologist and they're like, "Looks all good. It's a migraine. [Laughs.] What can we tell you?" ...

Zeller: Yeah.

Feltman: Is, is pretty wild to me.

Zeller: It's also interesting to me that, you know, for a lot of years, I mean, it was considered somewhat of a psychosomatic condition, or it was considered a vascular condition and just, "If we address the blood vessel tone, we might address this thing," when, in fact, there's all these clear indicators that it's a neurological event.

I mean, you're getting blurred vision. You're getting–some people get sleepy. Some people–I mean, obviously, there's a lot of nausea involved. The pain itself occurs on one side of the head. And yet it just was sort of overlooked for so many years. It's fascinating to me.

Feltman: And for listeners who don't know and maybe, like me a few years ago, are sort of blissfully ignorant of what it is we actually mean when we say migraine, could you tell us about those three big headache types and how they differ?

Zeller: Sure. So I think most people will experience a tension-type headache. That's sort of the biggest class of primary headache disorders. The thinking, I think, is that a large part of them are much more involved in sort of muscle tone and maybe even posture, and it tends to be sort of all around the head rather than on one side, which suggests that maybe it's not strictly an—a neurological disorder in the same way that migraine is.

I've had scientists tell me that they think a lot of tension-type headaches might actually be [a] migraine, so it's hard to draw these lines, but that would be the big category. And in most cases, not all—it can be incredibly debilitating—but in most cases tension-type headaches can be addressed with over-the-counter analgesics and maybe some lifestyle changes. Again, I don't want to, to belittle it because some people are really sort of bedeviled by these things, too.

But the next sort of most common primary headache is migraine. It affects women by an order of [about] three to one. It's typically one-sided. The word "migraine" itself comes from the Greek, which means "half the skull," and so that's where we get that word from. We can trace migraine's history back to the, you know, Egyptian papyri where we see it written about.

Not everyone experiences the other neurological symptoms that we just talked about, but definitely the pain, and it's almost always one-sided. And it's broken down by chronic or episodic. So they—if you get 15 of these headaches a month, you're considered chronic. If you get less—it's sort of arbitrary, but that's how they break it down.

But it can be really upending for people who have this, and whole seasons of their lives can be disrupted. It's often—there's high sensitivity to light and sound. People experiencing a migraine typically retreat to a dark room, put a pillow over their head and ride it out for however many hours, or sometimes days, that it might last.

The kind of headache that I have, cluster headache, is far more rare. Migraine affects about 15 percent of the population;

cluster is less than 1 [percent]. It's rather rare. It's *incredibly* painful and much more, I think, sort of attenuated than, then migraine.

The pain comes on incredibly fast. The severity of it is such that I couldn't even think of lying down; I mean, you, you sort of have to run around the room because it's almost like—the intensity is, like, akin to having your hand on a hot burner but not being able to take it off. [The pain is] much more short-lived. That pain will last—it'll come on in seconds and then last—almost like a stroke—and last for about an hour or two if you don't have an intervention and then go away.

It tends to come multiple times a day, and you'll have those attacks for one, two, maybe three months out of the year, and then they [makes vanishing noise] disappear. They just completely vanish, and you might not get them again for many months or even years in between. So unlike migraine, which I think people who have it sort of deal with it all the time, clusters come in clusters, and they come and go in ways that we don't understand and also are kind of fascinating if you can back up enough to look at it.

But those are the three main categories, yeah.

Feltman: And what surprised you the most in terms of things you learned while researching for the book?

Zeller: Well, I think the first thing that surprised me the most was just how little we know and it's as understudied as it is.

One thing that we didn't talk about is that, for as common as headache disorders are, med students get very little education in headache science at all. I talked to med students for the book who said, "You know, it came up in med school for about a half an hour once," and that was sort of all, despite there being [roughly] 50 million people in the United States alone with these things.

And I also talked to a lot of scientists who devote their lives to studying headache. I would say almost all of them were told as they were coming through school, "Don't focus your life on that. Don't focus your career on headache. There's no money in it. You can't help these people. It's not a very sexy thing to study. You should go into, like, movement disorders or Alzheimer's." So I was just sort of shocked that there's this ambient sort of bias against headache science even within the sciences. So that was pretty surprising to me.

Feltman: I mean, I find that disheartening [laughs] as somebody who deals with migraines. I imagine that was a little disheartening for you, too. But is there anything that you learned or came away from writing this book with that made you hopeful about, you know, the future of headache research?

Zeller: Yeah. I think the main thing is that there are people who are devoting their lives to studying these things, and, you know, I actually thought that anyone who was doing it probably had these disorders themselves, but that's not necessarily true. There are a lot of scientists around the world who are just really fascinated by this as a neurological disorder, who reckoned that if we could figure this out, it would really sort of, like, change people's lives. And in fact, I think that's true.

So there's a lot of nifty veins of science that are happening now. You probably have heard of the CGRP medications that came out. I think they hit the U.S. market in 2018. That came at the end of, like, 30 years of pretty intense and swashbuckling science that discovered these neurotransmitters. We talked about, like, neurochemicals sort of being elevated in the blood of people who are experiencing migraine—CGRP is one of those neurotransmitters, and we figured that out only in the 1990s. And then, you know, it took about 30 years to figure out, "What would happen if we produced a drug that blocked this neurotransmitter?" And in fact, in some large portion of trial patients it worked; it seemed to have a really great effect.

Now, when you sort of distribute those effects now on the market and look at it in aggregate, it's probably a lot like other medications in that it helps about half the people experience about half the number of headaches that they usually get, which, you know, that was another surprising thing to me in the book is to learn that, you know, 50 percent is, like, a home run when it comes to drug development [laughs]. If you're helping half the people, which for any particular person taking it is a roll of the dice, but as far as drug development goes it's a home run.

So the fact that those drugs are now on the market, and I spoke to a lot of people who are genuinely helped—and sometimes in a very, like, transformative way. Like, they spent decades just miserable and suddenly are sort of waking up into a life that's pain-free. It's sort of miraculous. It doesn't work for everyone, but I'm aware and know of lots of studies that are now looking at other neurotransmitters and other potential targets for new drugs.

So that's happening, and in a lot of ways this is a great time to be a headache suffer [laughs] because there's, there's a lot of exciting science going on.

Feltman: Well, thank you so much for coming on to chat with us. I'm sure a lot of listeners will be running out to check out the book.

Zeller: [Laughs.] Thanks for having me. I really appreciate it.

Feltman: That's all for today's episode. We're doing something a little different on Monday. I'm about to take a break from Science Quickly to go on parental leave, so I'm going to sit down and chat with our awesome interim host so you can get to know her. It's going to be a lot of fun!

Science Quickly is produced by me, Rachel Feltman, along with Fonda Mwangi and Jeff DelViscio. This episode was edited by Alex Sugiura. Shayna Posses and Aaron Shattuck fact-check our show. Our theme music was composed by Dominic Smith. Subscribe to *Scientific American* for more up-to-date and in-depth science news.

For *Scientific American*, this is Rachel Feltman. Have a great weekend!

About the Authors

Rachel Feltman is former executive editor of Popular Science *and forever host of the podcast* The Weirdest Thing I Learned This Week. *She previously founded the blog* Speaking of Science *for the* Washington Post.

Fonda Mwangi is an award-winning multimedia editor at Scientific American *and producer of* Science Quickly. *She previously worked at* Axios, *the* Recount *and* WTOP News. *She holds a master's degree in journalism and public affairs from American University in Washington, D.C.*

Alex Sugiura is a Peabody and Pulitzer Prize–winning composer, editor and podcast producer based in Brooklyn, N.Y. He has worked on projects for Bloomberg, Axios, Crooked Media *and Spotify, among others.*

Jeffery DelViscio is currently chief multimedia editor/executive producer at Scientific American. *He is former director of multimedia at* STAT, *where he oversaw all visual, audio and interactive journalism. Before that he spent more than eight years at the* New York Times, *where he worked on five different desks across the paper. He holds dual master's degrees in journalism and in Earth and environmental sciences from Columbia University. He has worked onboard oceanographic research vessels and tracked money and politics in science from Washington, D.C. He was a Knight Science Journalism Fellow at the Massachusetts Institute of Technology in 2018. His work has won numerous awards, including two News and Documentary Emmy Awards.*

Rising Physical Pain Is Linked to More 'Deaths of Despair'

By Lucía Macchia

Roughly 110,000 Americans died from a drug overdose between February 2021 and February 2022. That figure is part of a larger troubling trend. Overall life expectancy in the U.S. fell in 2020 and again in 2021, after decades of progress–and deaths linked to alcohol, drugs, and suicide are a major part of that change. (So are deaths from COVID, of course.) Overdoses, suicides and other "deaths of despair"–a label proposed by economists Anne Case and Angus Deaton–have been climbing since the 1990s and may have accelerated in recent years.

What exactly is driving this phenomenon, and what can be done to address it? To answer these urgent questions, many scholars are focusing on economic stress and psychological states such as depression and hopelessness. That approach makes sense: by definition, despair involves the absence of hope. Losing a job, recovering from an accident or illness, and experiencing divorce or financial difficulties may trigger desperation. People may use drugs and alcohol to ease these uncomfortable mental states.

But there is another important factor that studies of despair sometimes miss. Scientific evidence shows that one common denominator in this cycle of stress, anxiety, depression and substance abuse is physical pain. As a behavioral scientist, I study how socioeconomic, psychosocial and behavioral elements may contribute to pain. The findings from my work and others in this field suggest that tracking a community's physical aches and agonies is important.

The relationship between despair and pain is multifaceted. As most people know from personal experience, physical pain increases psychological distress and anxiety. Several studies have found that people with severe pain—as opposed to those with low or moderate pain—are more likely to worry about their affliction and its possible consequences. And pain may lead to poor sleep quality, which in turn increases the risk of anxiety and depression.

The reverse relationship is also possible: psychological distress can cause physical pain. For instance, job strain, anxiety caused by social discrimination, stressful family relationships and adverse experiences in early adulthood can exacerbate physical pain. Neuroscientists have even discovered a mechanism that could explain these findings. When someone is in a negative mood, researchers have found, the brain areas that play a role in physical pain also engage.

Lastly, physical pain is important when we consider the harmful behaviors involved in deaths of despair. For example, some people use drugs and alcohol to manage their pain. One 2020 study found that drug misuse was more strongly linked to physical pain than to poor mental health. For that matter, feeling severe or chronic pain can lead to self-harm or suicide.

The opioid epidemic may be the most prominent example of how physical pain and despair interact. The misuse of painkillers, especially opioids, generates changes in the brain that trigger higher pain sensitivity, as well as greater tolerance of and addiction to these drugs. As a result, people are more likely to overdose on these medications. At the same time, excessive use of drugs and consumption of alcohol can trigger physical pain that in turn reinforces the negative behavioral cycle of pain.

Taken together, research makes it clear that pain and despair are powerfully linked. Tracking pain can help doctors treat patients but can also help societies track well-being. Unfortunately, a central tool for this kind of research is falling out of favor. Many American physicians are challenging the use of self-reported pain assessments because these questionnaires sometimes prompt doctors to prescribe opioids. In fact, in 2016 the U.S. Centers for Medicare & Medicaid Services decided to remove some questions about pain medications from a national hospital survey for that reason. But losing these pain data also means losing crucial insights into people's needs, mental states and behaviors.

In addition, my research shows that understanding physical pain at a larger scale may be an essential step to confront rising deaths of despair. For example, using more than a decade of data from 146 countries, my colleague Andrew Oswald and I published a study in 2021 that showed that reports of physical pain were greater when the unemployment rate was high. We argue that recessions can create financial stress that in turn leads to greater physical pain. This idea has important implications. If deaths from despair in the U.S. map onto financial insecurity, policy makers need to think critically about how to help families cope with difficult economic times.

The U.S. is not the only country that stands to gain from such policies. Late last year I published an analysis using global data that found that physical pain has increased substantially in recent years. In 2009 one in four people around the world reported physical pain. Today one in three are in pain. Much like despair in the U.S., inequality adds a striking dimension to these data. My study found that the increase in physical discomfort is greatest among women, young people and individuals with less income or education. In response to these patterns, it is imperative that societies record and monitor pain data. Only then can we understand how to address these urgent trends.

About the Author

Lucía Macchia is a behavioral scientist at City, University of London. She studies the socioeconomic, psychosocial and behavioral determinants of physical pain. She has also written about pain for the Harvard Business Review.

The Mirror Cure for Phantom Pain

By Lorimer Moseley

In a previous, more adventurous stage of life, I hitchhiked around Australia. I got a lift out of Adelaide from a man with one leg, the other having been amputated after a car accident when he was six. There were two remarkable things about this man. The first was that he drove a manual - three pedals, one leg. The second was his remarkable method of gaining relief from an excruciating pain in his missing foot: he would put his prosthetic leg in the exact location he felt his own leg to be, and then drive a screwdriver into the painful spot. As long as he could see it, driving the screwdriver into the exact site of his pain turned it off just like a switch-he called it his 'magic button'. Either he was lying, or something about the screwdriver, and seeing the phantom limb, relieved his pain. I don't reckon he was lying.

Such phantoms of missing body parts are generated by the same brain mechanisms that generate the experience of an existing limb. Nearly everyone who has a limb amputated or the nerve supply removed reports experiencing some kind of phantom limb, but only some report persistent phantom limb pain. Those who do, however, report that the pain is very nasty - it is usually untouched by drugs or implanted pain relief devices. It would be ideal to find an inexpensive self-treatment that has almost no side effects, nor risks. Some think that such a treatment may be found in mirrors. Although 19th century neurologists, such as Pierre Janet, had experimented with the mirror treatment, modern versions of the treatment were developed by Vilayanur S. Ramachandran at the University of California, San Diego.

Fixing Phantom Pain

A recent letter by Jack Tsao, et. al in the New England Journal of Medicine describes one of the better attempts to elucidate the true value of mirror therapy for phantom limb pain. The researchers randomly assigned 22 lower-limb amputees with phantom limb pain to one of three groups:

1. Mirror movements: patients watched the reflected image of their intact foot in a mirror while they moved both feet simultaneously. (Obviously, amputees can't move their missing foot, but they can move their phantom foot.)
2. Covered mirror movements: patients performed the same movements but the mirror was covered so they did not see a moving limb.
3. Imagined movements: subjects mentally pictured moving the phantom foot, with eyes closed.

All patients performed 15 minutes per day of their assigned therapy and recorded the number, duration and intensity of pain episodes. After four weeks, there were two key findings. First, pain decreased significantly in all six patients doing the mirror movements, with the median decrease, as reported on a 100 point scale, being from 30/100 to about 5/100. Second, three out of six patients in the covered mirror movements group, and four out of six patients in the imagined movements group, got worse, not better.

Let's get the research questions out of the way first, and then get back to the potential importance of the study. I think it is a pity that this paper was a letter, because a letter's need for brevity meant that key information was left out. As a researcher, I want to know:

1. What happened to the three who didn't finish the study? Which group were they in? If they were all in the mirror group, then the results would be far less convincing.
2. To what question did the pain measure relate? If it related to pain at the end of the 15 minutes, then the study tells us about instantaneous effects. If it related to pain over the last few days or week, then the study gets more exciting.

3. How did they remove bias? Reporting bias is a big player in pain studies and could easily impart reductions in pain of 30/100.

Without the answers to those questions, and a few slightly more pedantic ones, it is very difficult to know what the study actually showed. However, let's give the authors the benefit of the doubt and presume that they actually did show that mirror movements decrease phantom limb pain. The most obvious next question is "Why?" The authors suggest that the effect might be due to activation of mirror neurons in the brain, which fire when we observe another person doing a movement, and presumably also when we observe ourselves doing a movement. I don't think this explains the result because these mirror neurons also fire when we move, which means they should have been firing during the other two conditions. The authors also suggest that "seeing" the missing limb move might deactivate systems that perceive certain types of pain, which, roughly interpreted, means that seeing the missing limb move might decrease phantom limb pain. Not an explanation so much as a restatement of the result.

What is Pain?

To consider how mirror movements might reduce pain, it might be helpful to first consider what pain is. I argue that pain emerges from the brain in accordance with the brain's unconscious perception of danger to the body part in question. Sensory input of danger (called nociception) is important, but not sufficient (nor necessary actually), for pain. Perhaps mirror movements simply convince the brain that all is exactly as it should be, which removes the brain's need to evoke pain. Alternatively, perhaps mirror therapy is a great distracter: distraction remains our most effective analgesic. Such explanations are very reasonable, but not particularly exciting.

Here is a more exciting theory, one the authors' introduction suggests they had in mind. It is based on the idea that phantom limb pain results from an internal conflict in the brain. Although sensory feedback, from the nerves that used to supply the missing limb, tells the brain that the limb is still present, visual feedback tells the brain it is not. According to that theory, seeing the phantom would remove the conflict and attempting to move the phantom (i.e. the other two conditions) might exacerbate it (although removing visual feedback didn't help, which doesn't fit neatly into the theory). That anaesthetizing the stump can eliminate phantom limb pain seems consistent with this theory. Perhaps anaesthetizing the stump brings sensory feedback into line with visual feedback, whereas mirror movements bring visual feedback into line with sensory feedback.

Of course, perhaps the key to mirror movements is seeing the movements, not necessarily seeing them in a mirror. A previous study in 14 lower limb amputees with phantom limb pain used a control condition in which patients watched the intact limb but couldn't see its reflection. There was no added benefit of seeing the phantom limb. However, that study looked at single sessions of ten movements each performed ten times, whereas the Chan et al. paper concerned four weeks of 15 minutes a day. Their data suggest that there is a cumulative effect, such as that observed with virtual walking, an approach that utilizes visual feedback to give paraplegic patients the perception that they are watching themselves walk. In my experience, patients don't get long-term relief from phantom limb pain by performing mirror movements. On that basis, I devised an alternative program that involved first doing implicit and then explicit motor imagery. Motor imagery refers to activation of the brain's movement-related processes without actually executing the movement. The same brain areas and processes underpin motor imagery and motor execution. The advantage of the former, however, is that it is not disrupted by an inability of the body to execute the command. The difference between implicit and explicit motor imagery is that you don't know you are doing the former, whereas you intentionally do the latter. The implicit imagery we used was a task in which we asked participants to judge whether a pictured hand was a left or a right hand. To determine the side, a person mentally maneuvers his or her own hand to match the posture of the one shown in the picture–but the person isn't aware of how the brain does it. The program progressed from implicit motor imagery to explicit motor imagery and then to mirror movements. That randomized controlled trial included patients with complex regional pain syndrome and showed long-term (six months) improvements that were similar in magnitude to those reported by Chan et al.

If there is a cumulative effect, then resolution of conflict between sensory and visual feedback is unlikely to be the key mechanism. Perhaps, then, mirror movements actually serve to correct faulty maps of the body part, which are held throughout the brain, most famously in the primary sensory cortex. We know the brain's map of the limb is disrupted in phantom limb pain; we know the map returns to normal when phantom limb pain resolves; and we know visual input of a body part can affect the body map. The disrupted body map theory seems worthy of investigation, but at the moment, we don't really know.

In summary, the article by Chan et al re-energizes the debate about mirrors and phantom limb pain. I don't think, in its published form, it proves an effect, but it does remind us that we need tight, well controlled, and well reported clinical trials. A cheap, safe and side-effect free treatment for what is a nasty and debilitating problem would be absolutely terrific.

Section 4: Healing Pain and Injuries

Heal Your Injuries Faster than Ever

By Lydia Denworth

After a slip on the ice, a sports injury, even surgery, most people's instinct is to rest what hurts. "When you have an acute injury, your body is sending signals through the peripheral and central nervous systems and the immune system to say, hold on, I need to stop doing this so we can allow the tissue to heal," says Ericka Merriwether, a physical therapist and pain researcher at New York University. Rest, after all, is the first part of the familiar RICE therapy, which stands for "rest, ice, compression and elevation."

But experts no longer believe RICE is the best strategy for recovery. They especially quibble with the first step: rest. Even Gabe Mirkin, the sports medicine physician who coined the RICE acronym in 1978, has acknowledged that newer evidence suggests other approaches are more effective.

Resting an injury can alleviate pain and may be necessary in the short term, especially for injuries such as muscle tears, which might be exacerbated by movement. In most cases, however, limiting movement does not promote healing. In fact, immobilization causes muscles to weaken and lose stability. An injured body part that is immobilized for too long is more likely to move from acute to chronic pain (that is, pain that lasts more than three months).

Instead of rest, "motion is the potion," experts say. And it is important to move far sooner than many imagine. Once a physician determines that movement is safe and that there's no biological reason not to engage in it, it's a case of "use it or lose it," says Rianne van Boekel, a nurse and associate professor at the Radboud University Medical Center in the Netherlands whose research focuses on acute and transitional pain.

Studies bear out the early-movement idea. In a controlled trial of athletes with serious soft-tissue injuries, researchers found that those who started rehabilitation two days after an injury instead of nine days later were able to return to sports 20 days sooner (in

63 days rather than 83). In a separate study, those who engaged in progressive agility training rather than static stretching were less likely to reinjure themselves. And in people with low back pain, consistent movement and exercise can improve pain levels, range of motion, strength and tissue repair.

That helps to explain why a popular acronym to emerge as a replacement for RICE is POLICE, in which the O and L stand for "optimal loading," or putting stress on tissues to induce the cellular changes that optimize recovery. (The other letters stand for "protection," "ice," "compression" and "elevation," so some parts of the RICE approach still hold.)

Putting stress on injured tissues does hurt, and the relation between pain and movement is complex. A person's responses to pain strongly influence their recovery from injury, researchers say, because the perception of pain has social and psychological elements as well as biological ones.

Injured tissue sends signals to the brain, which is where we perceive pain. "People say pain is in your head, and yes, it is," Merriwether says. There are also descending pain pathways from the brain back to the periphery of the body that inhibit and modulate the perception of pain.

That is why social environments and psychology play roles. Studies indicate that family caregivers might delay recovery if they do too much for an injured loved one, says anesthesiologist and pain researcher Esther Pogatzki-Zahn of the University of Münster in Germany. And, she says, people who must carry on with their lives–taking care of children or returning to work–often report lower levels of pain than people who don't. On the psychological front, anxiety is a major risk factor for developing chronic pain after an injury. The more someone fears pain, and the more they avoid moving because of it, the worse they usually become.

To encourage movement and the healing it can bring, pain experts are working to educate people. "Pain reduction is the goal," Pogatzki-Zahn says. In a 2025 randomized controlled trial of 150 people, nurses delivered one two-hour virtual lesson on pain and nonpharmacological ways to relieve it. Such approaches can include distraction, mindfulness and virtual-reality exercises. Patients who received the pain intervention scored significantly lower on measures of pain catastrophizing after eight weeks than those who were put on a wait list for the class. The first group also had better scores on pain intensity, depression, pain self-efficacy, fatigue and satisfaction with social roles. "The best way to deal with pain is to accept that you are in pain," van Boekel says.

Painkillers can also help, although the goal should be to take the least amount of medicine for the shortest time possible, van Boekel notes—"enough to be able to move, not to get rid of all the pain." And she advises taking acetaminophen (Tylenol) rather than ibuprofen (Advil) because it has no side effects at correct dosages.

Researchers are also paying closer attention to how pain is assessed. For instance, the latest studies suggest that clinical evaluations should more carefully distinguish between pain at rest and movement-evoked pain because it turns out patient outcomes can vary according to which type of pain they experience.

There is far more to understand about the role of pain and movement in recovery, but for now it seems fair to call on another familiar saying: no pain, no gain.

About the Author

Lydia Denworth is an award-winning science journalist and contributing editor for Scientific American. *She is author of* Friendship: The Evolution, Biology, and Extraordinary Power of Life's Fundamental Bond *(W. W. Norton, 2020) and several other books of popular science.*

How Much Do Our Thoughts Shape Our Health?

By Ellen Langer & Peter Aungle

Time heals all wounds, as the saying goes. But any medical professional can tell you that the hours required for recovery after an injury can vary widely. A person's age, lifestyle and level of social support, for example, are all known influences on how quickly their body heals.

Their thoughts can play a remarkably powerful role as well. In a recent experiment, we tested whether expectations about the time it takes to heal can affect how long it actually takes to recover. We found that people's perception of the passage of time influenced how quickly their wounds healed. The work is just the latest in a larger collection of evidence–documented in a new book written by one of us (Langer), *The Mindful Body*–that underscores the unity of mind and body, an idea with profound implications for health and well-being.

For the past 45 years, members of the Langer Lab have studied the ways in which the mind shapes the physiology of the body, or what our lab refers to as mind-body unity. The basic idea is simple: when people conceive of the mind and the body as a single entity rather than separable units, they can see how the mind has enormous control over health and well-being. Wherever we put our mind, so too will be our body.

The first test of this concept was the counterclockwise experiment, which one of us (Langer) designed and ran in 1979. In that study, elderly men lived in a retreat that was retrofitted to appear as if it had existed 20 years earlier and had vintage furniture, appliances and magazines. We asked the men to live as their younger self. They discussed past events in the present tense as if they were currently unfolding. The results were astonishing. Without any medical intervention, their hearing, vision, memory and strength improved. They also were perceived to look noticeably younger in photographs by the end of the week.

Since that time the Langer Lab has found further confirmation of mind-body unity. We have discovered that expecting fatigue can cause people to feel more tired and that thinking you will catch a cold is associated with an increased likelihood of doing so. In another study, people who anticipated certain benefits such as weight loss from daily exercise did see those benefits, even as other people doing the same activities without those expectations saw no such changes.

In the recent study of wound healing, we looked closely at how expectations could affect recovery from a physical injury. We recruited 33 participants to undergo a controlled procedure three times that left mild bruising on the skin. In each case, there was a 28-minute healing observation period, and during that time frame, we asked people to fill out a survey at specific intervals.

In two conditions, we manipulated the experience of time. For example, in a "fast time" condition, we told participants to respond to the survey every eight minutes, and we gave them a timer that–unbeknownst to them–ran at double speed. As a result, every actual minute corresponded to two minutes on the timer, such that the 28-minute total felt like a quick 56 minutes. In a "slow time" condition, the survey occurred every two minutes, and we set the timer to run at half its normal speed. In this setup, the 28-minute period felt like a glacial 14 minutes.

We found that wounds healed faster when participants believed more time had passed and slower when they believed less time had passed–even though the actual elapsed time was the same in every case. We are now in the process of replicating and extending this finding to people recovering from hernia surgery, cataract surgery and dental surgery.

Our implicit beliefs about time are not the only thing we can change to improve our health–our research suggests we should also think more mindfully about categories and diagnostic labels. For example, when we spoke with endocrinologists, they agreed that there was no relevant difference between someone who measured a

5.6 percent or 5.7 percent on a hemoglobin test called A1C, which measures blood sugar levels. But a line must be drawn somewhere, and standard medical protocol is to consider anyone with an A1C level below 5.7 percent as having "normal" levels and anyone above that point as "prediabetic." In a study that was recently accepted for publication, we compared data from 3,984 people who scored a 5.6 percent or 5.7 percent and found a significant difference in their ensuing medical trajectory. Those who got the prediabetic label experienced significantly greater increases in A1C results over the ensuing 10 yearsand had a significantly higher tendency to develop diabetes. Because the two groups were essentially the same at the start, the most reasonable conclusion is that subsequent differences were the result of the diagnostic label.

While it's worth noting that doctors may have treated these people differently once they received the prediabetic label, many endocrinologists told us that they generally give patients with either a 5.6 or 5.7 percent score the same advice: they note that the patient's blood glucose level is a little high and suggest that lifestyle changes could help. We therefore suspect people with this classification tended to have different expectations for themselves–even though, initially, people in both groups had comparable blood sugar levels on the high side of normal. We dubbed this tendency for otherwise comparable people to fall victim to the diagnostic label they are given "the borderline effect": when we set a threshold for a specific medical condition, people immediately above that borderline and those immediately below it may be essentially the same, but after the label is applied, they leave with very different impressions of their health.

Taken together, this work suggests that people can think themselves sick when they could otherwise be healthy and that they can also think themselves well. Each person goes through life acquiring various beliefs about how their body works and what it means to be healthy. Often these ideas reflect our core assumptions about the world and affect us with little conscious awareness. Much as someone can develop preferences or biases based on past experience, our research suggests that people also develop implicit beliefs that affect their health. For instance, a person may think they can spot the signs that they are getting sick or older. Their expectations, which structure how they feel, what they think and what they do, shape what happens next.

Going a step further, healthy living, which is undoubtedly a function of healthy choices, such as wearing sunscreen and brushing our teeth, is also a function of healthy thinking. As one of us (Langer) has argued for decades, most people act mindlessly most of the time because they are preoccupied with their past thoughts, which blinds them to the present. But we can notice and question our thoughts and implicit beliefs, especially when they're counterproductive–such as expecting to heal slowly or thinking we are just too frail to cope.

We can ask ourselves questions such as: How do we know that these ideas are accurate? What past experiences and situational factors might be unduly influencing our beliefs? Are there equally valid alternative beliefs to consider? And when we encounter a more constructive alternative that resonates, we can embrace it. Thoughts, feelings, and actions will then change accordingly. Just like that, better health is often only a thought away.

About the Authors

Ellen Langer is a professor of psychology at Harvard University who has earned three distinguished scientist awards and a Liberty Science Center Genius Award. Her most recent book, The Mindful Body: Thinking Our Way to Chronic Health, *presents, among other things, several studies on mind-body unity and its potential to improve health and well-being.*

Peter Aungle is a Ph.D. candidate in psychology at Harvard University. He is leading investigations into wound healing and the borderline effect. Peter's research explores the ways in which attention, beliefs and expectations interact to shape health over time.

Learning to Accept Discomfort Could Help You Thrive

By J. David Creswell

Can you imagine getting a root canal or other major dental procedure without novocaine? A scientist colleague of mine recently told me about a painful exposed nerve in his tooth. Rather than requesting a numbing option from his dentist, he used a "focus in" meditation technique to direct all his attention to his mouth with as much calming equanimity as he could muster. Doing so transformed the pain for a few minutes. Each time the dentist touched the tooth, my colleague felt bubbles of joy, and this feeling lasted until the dentist interrupted by asking, "Why are you smiling?"

A fair question is why anyone would want to be fully aware of intensely negative or painful experiences. But what might sound like a punishing choice–to embrace suffering or distress–may in some instances be helpful. A stream of scientific articles suggests that there are benefits in turning toward discomfort or upsetting emotions with acceptance. In addition, all of us can gain from finding ways to cope with stress and unhappiness–particularly when the circumstances are beyond our control. As a researcher who has studied meditation for more than 20 years, I believe that the cultivation of equanimity, a central element of certain mindfulness-meditation practices, can help.

It's important to first define the idea of turning toward discomfort. I'm not advocating for people to put themselves in dangerous or excruciating positions. But when we push ourselves into challenging or discomfiting situations, much like trainers who push athletes just past their comfort zone to make gains, learning often happens. Indeed, a 2022 study involving more than 2,000 people demonstrated that the participants who were explicitly encouraged to push themselves into awkward, uncomfortable situations across multiple domains–including taking improv classes to boost self-confidence and reading about opposing political viewpoints—later reported the greatest degree of personal growth.

Another study, published in 2023, found that people who can face negative emotions such as sadness and anger in a neutral way are more satisfied, are less anxious and have fewer symptoms of depression than those who judge their negative feelings harshly. That study aligns with a growing consensus in psychology that suggests we can learn powerful lessons about ourselves if we can sit with our emotions and thoughts with an open, curious mind.

My own research indicates that meditation provides an ideal way to practice turning toward discomfort—particularly when it improves one's equanimity. Broadly, mindfulness meditation is a form of mental training that helps people focus on attending to the present moment in an open and receptive way. "Equanimity" refers to a mental attitude of being at peace with the push and pull of experience. In my laboratory at Carnegie Mellon University, we conducted several clinical trials on developing equanimity during mindfulness-meditation training. This approach includes guided meditation exercises such as using a matter-of-fact voice to label uncomfortable sensations in the body and welcoming uncomfortable feelings by saying "yes" aloud each time a sensation is detected.

To gauge the effectiveness of such interventions, we recruited 153 stressed adults in Pittsburgh and offered them a mindfulness-meditation training program with or without training in equanimity. For example, the mindfulness-only group built skills to recognize ongoing experiences, whereas the equanimity group practiced acceptance of those experiences in addition to the basic recognition. Our equanimity training group had much better outcomes on several measures. After just 14 days of training, the participants who learned equanimity skills had significantly lower biological stress responses when asked to deliver a difficult speech and solve math problems in front of experts in white lab coats. The equanimity skills group also had lower blood pressure and hormonal stress levels.

In the days after training, people introduced to equanimity exercises reported significantly higher positive emotions and well-being throughout the day and more meaningful social interactions than participants who received mindfulness training without the equanimity component. It was as though developing an attitude of equanimity had transformed their emotional reactivity to stress, helping them better appreciate and savor daily life's many little positive experiences and making them more curious and open to connecting with others.

We are expanding on this work in several ways, including by developing an app that offers equanimity training on demand. We are also conducting trials with participants who have stress-related gastrointestinal disorders. Meanwhile other scientists are further exploring equanimity's power.

In 2022, for instance, researchers based in Australia published a study examining isolation and psychological distress in 578 people during the COVID pandemic. They found that the degree to which people felt alone during that period predicted their depression, anxiety and stress—but this dynamic could be mediated by equanimity. That is, people who reported higher levels of equanimity (based on how much they agreed or disagreed with statements such as "I experience a sense of mental balance regardless of what is happening in my life") reported less psychological distress even though they were feeling isolated. In other words, equanimity can be protective in a way that prevents feelings of social disconnection from leading to mental distress.

Equanimity can help us weather the inevitable periods of suffering that we all face at some point in our life. Many people are hurting and looking for ways to cope. Our social lives are suffering, too, which prompted the U.S. surgeon general to declare a national advisory last year about our surging epidemic of loneliness.

Without question, there are many important steps we need to take collectively to respond to these challenges—including looking closely at societal structures and choices that contribute to these problems. But we can each build resilience on a personal level by cultivating greater acceptance of our experience—good or bad, painful or pleasant—in the present moment.

About the Author

J. David Creswell is the William Dietrich II Chair Professor of Psychology and Neuroscience at Carnegie Mellon University and chief of science at Equa Health. His Health and Human Performance Laboratory studies what makes people resilient under stress, the science of mindfulness meditation training, and wellness.

Section 5: Pain Relievers and How They Work

Toward Better Pain Control

By Allan Irwin Basbaum & David Julius

Throbbing, itching, aching, stabbing, stinging, pounding, piercing. Pain comes in a range of unpleasant flavors. But all pain has one thing in common: those who endure it want it to stop.

Yet the most widely used analgesics today are essentially folk remedies that have served for centuries: morphine and other opiates derive from the opium poppy, and aspirin comes from willow bark. Although these treatments can give relief, each has its limitations. Aspirin and other nonsteroidal anti-inflammatory drugs (NSAIDs), such as ibuprofen, cannot ease the most severe types of discomfort. And even opiates, generally the strongest medicines, do not work for everyone. Moreover, they can have serious side effects, and patients tend to become tolerant to them, requiring escalating doses to get any relief at all.

Over the past 20 years neurobiologists have learned a great deal about the cellular circuits and the specialized molecules that carry pain signals. Today this knowledge is being exploited to devise new strategies for managing pain better and causing fewer side effects. Indeed, more approaches than we have room to dicuss are now under study.

Particles of Fire

In the 17th century French philosopher René Descartes enumerated a theory to explain how people sense pain. In his view, a pinch, a whack or a poke essentially tugged on a neural rope that then rang a pain alarm bell in the brain. Imagine, for example, burning a foot. "Fast moving particles of fire," Descartes thought, would create a disturbance that "passes along the nerve filament until it reaches the brain."

Descartes was not too far off. Pain generally begins at the periphery: in the skin, an internal organ or any other site outside the central nervous system (CNS)—that is, outside the brain and spinal cord. Stubbing a toe or leaning against a hot stove activates neurons (nerve cells) called nociceptors that respond specifically to hurtful stimuli, such as extreme temperature or mechanical pressure, or to chemicals generated in response to injury or inflammation.

Nociceptors have two arms: a sensation-detecting branch that projects out to the periphery, where it innervates small patches of tissue, and a second branch that extends into the spinal cord [see box below]. The neuron's cell body, which resides in a structure outside the spine, sits between the two. When specialized detector molecules on the peripheral branch encounter a noxious agent in the skin or an organ, they trigger an impulse that travels up the line, along the central branch and on to an area of the spinal cord known as the dorsal horn. There the nociceptor releases signaling molecules called neurotransmitters that activate neurons in the dorsal horn, prompting them to transmit the alarm message up to the brain. Although nociceptors are often called pain-sensing neurons, they merely indicate the presence of potentially harmful stimuli; it is the brain that interprets the signal as painful and prompts us to say "ouch."

Not all pain is worrisome. For example, the acute kind that accompanies a minor tissue injury such as a sprain or abrasion is protective: it encourages an organism to avoid further injury. This kind tends to be temporary and to subside over time.

The pain that most troubles patients—and doctors—fails to disappear and is difficult to treat. In many cases, the problem arises because the injury or the inflammation that triggers the discomfort persists. The aches of arthritis result from ongoing inflammation, and the agony that can accompany invasive cancer stems to a large extent from tissue injury and inflammation.

In other cases, persistent pain is neuropathic, resulting from damage to nerve cells themselves. It can develop when neurons in the CNS sustain damage from multiple sclerosis, a stroke or spinal cord injury, for example. Or it can derive from injury to peripheral neurons. Amputees who endure aching in a limb that is no longer there (phantom limb pain) and people who feel burning in their skin for years after a herpes infection has subsided (postherpetic neuralgia) are all suffering from neuropathic pain. When this kind of hurt continues, it is not symptomatic of some ongoing injury or another disease; it is itself a disease of the nervous system and requires the attention of a pain specialist.

Pain without End

A major common denominator in those who suffer from hard-to-manage pain is abnormal sensitivity to stimuli. This sensitivity can take the form of hyperalgesia (an excessive reaction to typically painful inputs) or allodynia (pain in response to normally innocuous inputs). In those affected by allodynia, even the gentle pressure of clothing against one's skin or bending a joint can become unbearable.

Biologists now understand that such heightened sensitivity—or sensitization— stems from molecular or structural changes in nerve cells. In the periphery, for instance, molecules that promote inflammation may cause the nociceptors that detect noxious stimuli to become overly reactive to those inputs. Inflammatory molecules can even cause nociceptors to begin generating signals in the absence of any environmental input.

Sensitization can also result from CNS changes that lead to hyperactivity of pain-transmission pathways. The changes, which may persist for a long time, can include display of increased numbers of the receptors that respond to the neurotransmitters released by nociceptors and might even include rewiring of connections and a loss of nerve cells that normally inhibit pain signaling. When the CNS is involved, the condition is termed central sensitization.

Regardless of which specific processes are at fault, ongoing pain, it turns out, can lead to sensitization and thus exacerbate and prolong discomfort. Many researchers, therefore, have amelioration of hyperalgesia and allodynia foremost in their minds as they hunt for new analgesics. Meanwhile patients need to realize that persistent pain should not be borne stoically; it requires aggressive treatment to prevent further sensitization.

Start at the Beginning

In the search for new analgesics, much effort has been directed toward the place where hurtful signals typically originate: the periphery. Certain of the specialized molecules that nociceptors use to detect noxious stimuli rarely occur elsewhere in the body. Blocking these molecules would presumably shut off pain signaling without disrupting other physiological processes and, thus, without causing unwanted side effects.

Today's most popular remedies–aspirin and other NSAIDs–largely work their magic in the periphery. When a tissue is injured, a variety of cells in the area pump out chemicals called prostaglandins, which act on the pain-sensing branches of nociceptors, lowering their activation threshold. Aspirin and NSAIDs inhibit the activity of a family of enzymes (cyclooxygenases) that cells use to generate the pain-inducing prostaglandins. These over-the-counter compounds relieve everyday aches and pains. But they also inhibit prostaglandin production elsewhere in the body, often causing such side effects as stomach pain, diarrhea and ulcers. These problems can prevent the drugs' long-term use and limit the doses that can be given.

To reduce the gastrointestinal consequences, pharmaceutical companies developed a family of drugs that target the enzyme cyclooxygenase-2 (COX-2). Because COX-2 does not normally operate in the stomach or intestinal tract, blocking its activity should not cause the same disruptions as traditional NSAIDs do. Whether they are in fact gentler on the stomach remains to be established. In the meantime, the drugs have problems of their own. Rofecoxib (Vioxx), a COX-2 inhibitor that had been prescribed for relief of arthritis pain, was removed from the market when it was found to boost the risk of heart attack and stroke. Other COX-2 inhibitors are also being scrutinized for ill effects.

Send in the Salsa

Discovery of targets that reside almost exclusively on nociceptors provided an opportunity to develop drugs that act selectively to relieve pain. A particularly appealing one is the capsaicin receptor. This ion channel, present in the membrane of many nociceptors, responds not only to capsaicin, the pungent ingredient in chili peppers, but also to distressful heat and to protons (the hydrogen ions that make substances acidic); protons are unusually abundant in inflamed tissue. In the presence of these chemicals or of temperatures above 43 degrees Celsius, the channel allows sodium and calcium ions to flood into the nociceptor, stimulating it to generate a signal that translates into the burning sensation induced by heat, inflammation or spicy food.

Substances that inhibit the capsaicin receptors should therefore dampen inflammatory pain. Indeed, in laboratory animals, such "antagonists" have been able to relieve the very severe pain caused by the acidic environment around tumors that have metastasized to and damaged bone tissue. Today many pharmaceutical companies are competing to develop capsaicin receptor antagonists.

The possibilities for manipulating the receptor do not end there. Ironically, in some instances, purposely stimulating capsaicin receptors can alleviate pain. Topical creams containing capsaicin are being prescribed to relieve the itching, prickling and stinging sensations that can accompany postoperative wound healing or nerve impairments stemming from HIV infection, bouts of herpes and diabetes. Exactly how the ointments work is unclear, although small doses over time might ultimately make the receptor less responsive to the usual stimuli or might cause depletion of the neurotransmitters emitted by nociceptors.

Block Other Channels

A different kind of molecule found on the peripheral terminals of nociceptors is also attracting interest as a drug target. All neurons possess sodium channels that open in response to changes in the voltage across the nerve cell membrane, generating the impulses that relay messages from one neuron to the next. Local anesthetics that temporarily inactivate such voltage-gated sodium channels currently treat a variety of different pains, particularly those arising from a trip to the dentist. The problem, though, is that those anesthetics have to be applied at the site of the discomfort: disabling sodium channels throughout the nervous system could be fatal.

Pain-sensing neurons, however, possess a subclass of voltage-gated sodium channels, known as the TTX-resistant type, that do not occur in the CNS. Investigators therefore hope that drugs able to block this subclass could be administered systemically (throughout the body) without ill effects. Moreover, studies suggest that such agents could well dampen inappropriate hyperactivity by injured peripheral nerves and thus might relieve some neuropathic pain. Unfortunately, the pharmaceutical industry has so far been unable to successfully develop selective inhibitors for such channels, in part because they closely resemble TTX-sensitive sodium channels, which appear widely throughout the nervous system.

The channels could perhaps be selectively removed, however, with a new technique called RNA interference. The method relies on introducing into an organism tiny molecules known as small AMADEO BACHAR interfering RNAs (siRNAs). These siRNAs prevent the production of an unwanted protein by inducing the degradation of the molecules (messenger RNAs) that direct the protein's synthesis. The technique is being studied in humans for certain retinal conditions, but turning RNA interference into a pharmacological intervention for pain will be challenging. As is true of gene therapy, a virus will most likely be needed to deliver siRNA, and this aspect has raised safety concerns. Time will tell whether the approach will be practical as a pain therapy, but it remains an exciting possibility.

Suppose drug companies do develop a so-called magic bullet analgesic: a compound that specifically and effectively eliminates the activity of one of the pain-transducing molecules on nociceptors. Would this intervention provide relief from intractable pain? Maybe not, because closing off a single entrance to the pain pathway might not be enough.

Imagine, for example, a pharmaceutical that knocks out the receptor for bradykinin—a small protein, or peptide, that is produced during inflammation in the periphery. Bradykinin powerfully stimulates nociceptors, and an antagonist that blocks its receptors would certainly prevent those receptors from activating nociceptors. But it would not stop the neurons from recognizing and responding to other pain-inducing molecules generated by injury or inflammation—protons, prostaglandins, and a protein called nerve growth factor, for example. Similarly, hobbling only the capsaicin receptors might not mitigate all proton-mediated pain, because under certain circumstances, protons activate a separate population of detectors, called ASICs (acid-sensing ion channels), on nociceptors.

Focus on the Cord

One way around this redundancy problem would be to administer a cocktail of inhibitory molecules that targets multiple pain mechanisms. Another approach, though, would target molecules that act more centrally, blocking the ability of all nociceptors—no matter what stimuli initially activated them—to pass their pain signals to spinal cord neurons.

Morphine and other opiates, which bind to opioid receptors on the nociceptor endings that reach into the spinal cord, employ this latter tactic. In activating these receptors, opiates prevent neurotransmitter release, thus blocking the transmission of the pain message to spinal cord neurons. They also render dorsal horn neurons less able to respond to pain signals. Because these drugs act in the spinal cord, they should in theory be able to treat all types of pain, although they tend to work best against those related to inflammation.

Unfortunately, opioid receptors are present on neurons throughout the body, including in the brain and the gastrointestinal system. This ubiquity explains why morphine and its cousins can generate a broad set of undesirable side effects, including severe constipation and respiratory shutdown. These problems can restrict the amount of drug a patient can take safely or that a doctor will prescribe. And many physicians are reluctant to prescribe opiates for fear patients will become addicted. Addiction, however, is not common in those who take opiates only for pain. In part to avoid some of the undesirable effects, opiates are often delivered directly into the fluid-filled space around the spinal cord (intrathecally). The medicines may also be administered by injection (for postoperative pain) or via an indwelling pump (for chronic pain).

Alternatives to opiates are available as well. Medicines that interfere with calcium channels can prevent the release of neurotransmitters from nociceptor endings in the spinal cord. Gabapentin (Neurontin), an anticonvulsant, is believed to relieve some forms of pain by interacting with a specific subunit of certain calcium channels. And a relatively new drug called ziconotide (Prialt)—derived from the venom of a Pacific Ocean cone snail—inhibits a different variety of calcium channel known as the N-type.

Like opioid receptors, N-type calcium channels occur throughout the nervous system. If ziconotide were delivered systemically, blood pressure would decline precipitously. So the compound is administered intrathecally. Although the toxin blocks pain, its action within the CNS can still generate unpleasant side effects, including dizziness, nausea, headache and confusion. Ziconotide, therefore, is given mostly to patients with late-stage cancer who cannot get relief another way.

Recently drugs that act on cannabinoid receptors—the ones that mediate marijuana's effects—have been advancing through clinical trials. These agents seem to ease pain in several ways, including by interfering with signal transmission between nociceptors and their target cells and by reducing the activity of inflammatory cells.

Batten Down the Hatches

Some investigators are concentrating on preventing spinal neurons from responding to neurotransmitters released by nociceptors—particularly to the amino acid glutamate, the primary carrier of the pain message. Glutamate activates various receptors in the dorsal horn of the spinal cord. Of these, the NMDA class participates in central sensitization, which makes it a logical target for new analgesics.

Every neuron in the body possesses some type of NMDA receptor. Consequently, inhibiting all types at once would elicit catastrophic effects, including memory loss, seizures and paralysis. To avoid such reactions, researchers are attempting to hobble the receptor by acting on versions found mostly in the dorsal horn. Compounds that bind to a form containing what is called the NR2B subunit have yielded encouraging results in animal studies. For example, mice that had an NR2B inhibitor delivered directly into the spinal fluid were less sensitive to pain than were untreated animals. The drug also reversed allodynia in mice that had a peripheral nerve injury.

A number of nociceptors also release peptide neurotransmitters, such as substance P and calcitonin gene–related peptide (CGRP). These peptides activate pain-transmission neurons in the spinal cord by acting on discrete receptors, so drugs that bar interaction with those receptors would be expected to be helpful. Regrettably, selective blockade of the receptor used by substance P—the neurokinin-1, or NK-1, receptor—has failed in clinical trials for pain, perhaps because blocking that receptor by itself is insufficient. Whether quieting CGRP activity in the spinal cord will shut down pain is unknown, although the pharmaceutical industry is developing antagonists that aim to ease the agony of migraines by interfering with the release of CGRP onto blood vessels on the surface of the brain.

Kill the Messenger?

If all attempts to modulate pain signaling fail, one can consider killing the messenger. Cutting nociceptive nerves, though, generally backfires because, as we have noted, nerve injury can promote the onset of even more stubborn, persistent pain. Severing pathways in the spinal cord that convey information to the brain (cordotomy) was once common but now is reserved for terminal cancer patients unresponsive to all pain treatments. The problem with this last procedure is that the surgeon can not selectively cut the "pain" pathways.

A possible solution, now drawing considerable attention because of its success in animals, is a molecular therapy that takes out a subset of the spinal cord neurons receiving input from nociceptors. This cell-killing therapy couples saporin, a toxin, to substance P. The substance P in the conjugate binds to NK-1 receptors, leading to internalization of the whole compound, after which the saporin is freed to kill the neuron. Because the conjugate can enter only cells having an NK-1 receptor, researchers hope that side effects will be limited.

Ablation of neurons in the spinal cord, however, should be considered a method of last resort: neurons in the CNS do not grow back, so the resulting changes–for better or worse–will be permanent. The same permanence does not hold in the peripheral nervous system, where cut fibers can regenerate. Ideally, therapies that trim back the signal-detecting branches of nociceptors–such as high doses of capsaicin–would halt pain but allow the branches to grow back eventually, restoring normal pain detection to the patch of tissue innervated before.

Targeting neurons may not be the sole way to overcome pain. Studies indicate that glia, the cells that nurture neurons in the CNS, swing into action in response to damage to peripheral nerves. The glia migrate to the region of the dorsal horn associated with the injured nerves. Then the glia discharge a bevy of chemicals that prod nociceptor terminals to release neurotransmitters in the cord, thus perpetuating a pain signal. Some of these substances, including growth factors and molecules known as cytokines, also make dorsal horn neurons overly excitable, and drugs blocking that hyperactivity should help undercut excessive sensitivity. Various groups are working to identify—and find ways to inhibit—the molecules that recruit and activate glia when nerves are damaged.

Interestingly, prostaglandins are among the key substances released from activated glia in the spinal cord. There they enhance pain by blocking receptors for glycine on dorsal horn neurons. Glycine, an inhibitory neurotransmitter, normally quiets these neurons. NSAIDs may therefore work not only by interfering with the production of prostaglandins in the periphery (the familiar way) but also by inhibiting COX enzymes in glia. In that case, direct delivery of COX inhibitors into the spinal fluid might minimize the side effects caused by systemic delivery. A pharmaceutical that enhanced glycine receptor activity could also help tamp the transmission of pain messages to the brain.

A Question of Perception

In this article we have discussed a subset of the experimental approaches to treating pain, all of which have shown promise in animal studies. Those evoking the greatest excitement leave normal sensation intact while diminishing the heightened sensitization characteristic of the difficult-to-treat inflammatory and neuropathic pains and have an acceptable side-effects profile. But will these therapies help patients? And will they work on all types of pain? These questions remain unanswered.

One approach that deserves further exploration is the use of behavioral, nondrug therapies for intractable pain—particularly that associated with conditions such as fibromyalgia and irritable bowel syndrome, for which no one has conclusively established an organic cause. Roughly a decade ago researchers at McGill University demonstrated that hypnosis could alter brain activity along with a person's perception of pain. The scientists hypnotized volunteers and suggested to them that the hot water bath in which they had immersed their hands was either more unpleasant or less unpleasant than it really was.

Using positron-emission tomographic scanning to monitor brain activity, the investigators found that the somatosensory cortex, which responds to the magnitude of the physical stimulus, was equally active in both situations. But a second brain region, the cingulate cortex, was more active when subjects believed that the stimulus was more unpleasant, suggesting that hypnosis changed the way these individuals perceived sensations. By learning more about how the brain modulates the pain experience, investigators might be able to develop better cognitive therapies for moderating pain perception.

Poet Emily Dickinson often contemplated pain. In one work, she noted:

> Pain has an element of blank;
> It cannot recollect
> When it began, or if there were
> A day when it was not.
> It has no future but itself.

We can only hope continued research into the mechanisms of pain sensation will lead to safe, effective treatments that will alter pain's future, such that it reverts to a time when it was not.

About the Author

Allan Irwin Basbaum is professor and chair of the Department of Anatomy at the University of California, San Francisco. He is a Fellow of the American Academy of Arts and Sciences.

David Julius is professor and chair of the Department of Physiology at University of California, San Francisco and holds the Morris Herzstein Chair in Molecular Biology and Medicine. He is a member of the National Academy of Sciences and the American Academy of Arts and Science and has won numerous honors and awards, including the 2021 Nobel Prize in Physiology or Medicine.

Why the Pain Drug That Killed Prince Can Be Especially Dangerous

By Stephani Sutherland

Many questions still remain about the tragic and untimely death of musician and cultural icon Prince, but a report released last Thursday by the Anoka County, Minn., Midwest Medical Examiner's Office answered a big one: Prince's death was caused by an accidental overdose of the powerful opioid drug fentanyl. Little is known for certain about the circumstances leading up to his death but it now appears that, like millions of Americans, Prince was taking opioids to manage chronic pain.

Fentanyl is an opioid drug—a chemically synthesized relative of opiates such as morphine and heroin, which are derived from the opium poppy. The drugs mimic our brains' own pain-regulating molecules called endogenous opioids, which act at receptors found throughout the nervous system. All opioid drugs have the ability to dampen pain. In fact, opioids are so good at relieving pain that they are considered the gold standard against which all other analgesic drugs are measured. But that relief comes with significant risks. Opioids carry a range of side effects, the most severe of which apparently took Prince's life: death by respiratory depression, meaning that he stopped breathing.

"In a way, Prince is a poster child for what can happen with chronic use—and increasing doses—of these very powerful drugs," says Gary Franklin, a researcher at the University of Washington and medical director of the Washington State Department of Labor and Industries. Franklin speculates that Prince, like so many others, may have been being treated with opioids for chronic pain and developed tolerance—meaning that over time higher and higher doses are required to achieve the same pain relief. As doses escalate, so do risks. "It turns out that it doesn't take long to develop physical dependence, which means that when you try to cut back on the dose, you get withdrawal symptoms. It's a vicious cycle," Franklin adds.

If Prince had built up tolerance to opioids, how did he die of an overdose? The specific drug–fentanyl–found in Prince's body is particularly powerful; it is 100 times more potent than morphine. For example, the effects of a standard 10-milligram dose of morphine can be achieved with just 100 micrograms of fentanyl. Among opioid drugs, fentanyl is particularly fast-acting, which can make it more lethal in some situations.

Prince had a long history of clean, drug-free living, suggesting that he would not use street drugs. However, fentanyl is often mixed with heroinor other drugs and sold illegally, which accounts for many of the other deaths in which it is involved–as users may be unaware that their heroin is cut with the stronger drug. And pharmaceutical fentanyl was once prescribed only for severe short-term pain, such as after surgery, but patients are increasingly receiving it to manage chronic pain, often in a patch that delivers the drug through the skin. Fentanyl is also administered in lollipop form, typically to terminal cancer patients with otherwise untreatable pain. Whatever the source, "we don't know if Prince took the drug as directed or in excess," says Lynn Webster, a pain and addiction specialist based in Salt Lake City and past president of the American Academy of Pain Medicine.

The death certificate did not name any other drugs in his system but a number of medications–from other types of opioids to sleeping pills–would have increased fentanyl's risks in any user. Prince's small stature–the medical report listed him as 1.6 meters and 50 kilograms at death–did not likely contribute to an overdose death, according to Webster. "Most people who die from respiratory depression–they go to sleep and don't wake up," Franklin says. "This was different in the sense that he [presumably] passed out while awake" in the elevator where he was found an estimated six hours after his death.

Despite the fact that Prince died of an overdose of an opioid drug, whether or not he might have been addicted is another matter. "I'm not so sure he was addicted," Webster says. "I have not seen evidence that he was addicted." An opioid user can develop tolerance and even physical dependence on the drugs without being addicted. Less than 10 percent of patients taking opioids for chronic pain develop addiction in the classical sense, Webster says.

Prince's plane did make an emergency landing a few days before his death in order to get a life-saving dose of Narcan, or naloxone, a drug that counteracts opioids and can prevent overdose death. "The fact that he had already had an overdose episode–when death is prevented once by naloxone–that indicates big trouble," Franklin says.

About the Author

Stephani Sutherland is a neuroscientist and science journalist based in southern California. She wrote about the causes of long COVID in our March 2023 issue. Follow her on X @SutherlandPhD

What Is Journavx, the New Opioid-Free Painkiller from Vertex?

By Allison Parshall

For the first time in 25 years, the U.S. Food and Drug Administration has approved a new type of painkiller. Suzetrigine, sold as Journavx, is administered twice daily in 50-milligram oral tablets to treat moderate and severe acute pain.

Clinical trials showed that the medication dampened pain as effectively as an opioid-based painkiller. And perhaps most importantly, suzetrigine does so without the same risk of addiction.

How Does Suzetrigine Work?

The drug dampens pain signals before they reach the brain. It prevents nerve cells all over the body from firing by obstructing so-called sodium ion channels. These channels are embedded in a nerve cell's membrane, and by opening and closing, they carry electrical impulses along the nerve.

Drug companies have been trying to create painkillers that target sodium ion channels for decades, but the development pipeline had largely dried up after many false starts. With suzetrigine, developed by pharmaceutical company Vertex, they finally succeeded.

The FDA's approval is based on two phase 3 clinical trials conducted in patients after tummy tuck and bunion removal surgeries. In both trials, about 1,000 patients received suzetrigine, placebo, or the combination of the opioid hydrocodone and acetaminophen formerly sold as Vicodin. Suzetrigine and the opioid treatment both cut pain by about three points on the standard 10-point pain rating scale. Suzetrigine worked faster and had fewer side effects.

Why is Suzetrigine so Important?

For decades, people experiencing pain have had two options. One has been over-the-counter medications that offer limited relief, including acetaminophen and nonsteroidal anti-inflammatory drugs (NSAIDS) such as aspirin and ibuprofen. The other has been opioids, with their risk of addiction and adverse side effects. These limited options have made opioids the only choice for many people who experience serious pain, whether acute or chronic, and it has fueled an opioid crisis that kills more than 100,000 people in the U.S. each year and ravages communities.

Suzetrigine, along with similar new medications that are now being tested, will provide a much needed third option for people who seek pain relief. Because the drug works only on peripheral nerve cells and not on the brain or spinal cord, it does not carry the risk of addiction that opioids do.

While suzetrigine is only approved to treat acute pain, Vertex has reported positive results from a trial of the drug's safety and efficacy in people who experience chronic pain from diabetic peripheral neuropathy. A phase 3 clinical trial is now underway. Other companies are also working to develop medications that target sodium ion channels in different ways.

"We are definitely hopeful that we can replace opioids, and that's the goal here," said Ana Moreno of Navega Therapeutics to journalist Marla Broadfoot in a recent *Scientific American* feature article on the promise of these sodium-ion-channel-blocking drugs.

What are the Side Effects of Suzetrigine?

Among trial participants, the most common side effects of the drug were itching, muscle spasms, increased levels of creatine phosphokinase in the blood and rash. The medication should not be taken alongside others that strongly inhibit an enzyme called CYP3A, which includes some antibiotics and antivirals. People on suzetrigine should also not eat grapefruit.

Vertex says that the medication will be available for $15.50 per 50-milligram pill, or about $30 per day. In contrast, comparable doses of the hydrocodone and acetaminophen combination retail for an average of about $7 per day. It remains to be seen how insurance companies and Medicare will cover suzetrigine.

About the Author

Allison Parshall is associate editor for mind and brain at Scientific American *and she writes the weekly online Science Quizzes. As a multimedia journalist, she contributes to* Scientific American's *podcast* Science Quickly. *Parshall's work has also appeared in* Quanta Magazine *and Inverse. She graduated from New York University's Arthur L. Carter Journalism Institute with a master's degree in science, health and environmental reporting. She has a bachelor's degree in psychology from Georgetown University.*

Understanding Suzetrigine, a New Drug That Treats Pain at the Periphery

By Rachel Feltman, Marla Broadfoot & Fonda Mwangi

Rachel Feltman: Almost all humans experience pain in some form or another during their lives. And for many folks pain is a frequent or even constant companion. A National Institutes of Health study published last year reported that about 21 percent of U.S. adults experienced chronic pain in 2020. And while there are many medications out there to help people cope with pain, they can often cause their own headaches, to say the very least.

Now a pharmaceutical company is potentially on the cusp of releasing a brand-new type of pain medication—one that works to block pain signals like opioids do but without impacting the brain or spinal cord in ways that can lead to addiction.

For *Science Quickly*, I'm Rachel Feltman. I'm joined today by Marla Broadfoot, a freelance science journalist who recently covered the new drug for *Scientific American*.

Marla, thank you so much for joining us today.
Marla Broadfoot: Happy to be here.

Feltman: So let's start with a, a pretty basic question, though I think kind of a complicated one, too: When we talk about pain, what is it physiologically?

Broadfoot: Yeah, that's a great question. So pain is an unpleasant sensation—often an extremely unpleasant sensation—that is typically there to tell us that there's something wrong with your body. But then we feel pain, in cases of chronic pain, where there isn't anything wrong.

And so physiologically speaking, our body is home to lots and lots of these pain-sensing nerve cells that act like an alarm system. So they'll detect danger in the form of extreme temperatures or sharp objects or noxious chemicals. And then it'll send signals down nerve fibers to our spinal cord and up to our brain, and that's where pain becomes a reality.

And scattered all along these nerve fibers are these sodium channels, which are basically cellular gates that allow the influx of sodium ions to generate those electrical currents that are responsible for nerve impulses. And that's what these drugs that are being developed now are targeting.

Feltman: Yeah, well, and I'm excited to get into these new painkillers that you wrote about for *SciAm*. But just so that people have the context they need to understand: How do the pain relievers that are available to us today work, generally speaking?

Broadfoot: Yeah, so a lot of the pain relievers we use today are based on natural compounds that have been around for thousands of years.

So we all know about aspirin. The compounds in aspirin were derived from willow bark. And then we know about morphine and opioids. Those are derived from the opium poppy plant. And so these work not terribly specifically. So in the case of these nonsteroidal anti-inflammatories or NSAIDs—like ibuprofen, or Advil—those are targeting inflammation. And so I tweaked my back the other day. It hurts, probably because it was a bit of an injury. And so in that case, those drugs are trying to stop the production of the chemicals that cause inflammation and the associated pain.

And opioids work differently. So opioids are changing the brain's perception of pain. And they're doing that by targeting opioid receptors that are in the brain, in the spinal cord, in various parts of your body. And so those activate reward centers, can give you this feeling of pleasure, and that's often what makes them so addictive.

Feltman: So let's talk about this new painkiller. What is it called, who's making it, and how is it different from what we already have available?

Broadfoot: So this new pain drug is being made by Vertex Pharmaceuticals. It was called VX-548 for quite some time while it was under development. Now they're calling it suzetrigine.

And so it is–works differently than these other pain drugs out there. It could be, if it's FDA-approved, the first of a new class of pain medications. And so what it's doing is it's targeting these sodium channels that are scattered along our nerve cells in our periphery. And because it's targeting the periphery and stopping pain signaling there, they would not have the same addictive potential as compounds that are targeting your brain or spinal cord or your central nervous system.

Feltman: Very cool. So I know you got into this a little bit, but can we talk a little bit more about some of the upsides and downsides of the different kinds of pain medications that we currently have?

Broadfoot: Yeah, I mean, I think all the pain meds, one thing you're trying to do is balance safety and effectiveness. And so when you're talking about acetaminophen and Tylenol or ibuprofen and Advil, those are relatively safe compounds, relatively safe drugs, but they kind of have a ceiling, and so they're not necessarily as effective. Then you have opioids, which can be really strong and effective and potent–not in everybody, but they can be quite effective. But then they carry the risk of, you know, addiction, and as we've seen with the opioid epidemic, that's a very real risk.

Feltman: Yeah, so how could this new painkiller potentially solve some of those problems?

Broadfoot: Yeah, so the developers believe, and some other researchers I spoke to agree, that this new compound could kind of bridge the gap between those safer and perhaps less powerful medications that are over the counter like acetaminophen and these riskier but stronger medications like opioids. And they seem to work almost as if not the same effectiveness as some of the opioid combinations that are out there.

Feltman: It seems kind of wild to me that, you know, this would be the first new class of painkiller in so long, given that pain is such a universal problem for people, you know, at least at some time in their life, even if they don't deal with chronic, ongoing pain. What is it about pain as a problem or how the pharmaceutical industry approaches it that has kept new kinds of drugs from coming to market?

Broadfoot: Now that's a great question. So there's a number of reasons why it's been really hard to develop new pain medications.

One of them is just the nature of pain. So unlike with other conditions like diabetes–if you were to do a clinical trial for a new diabetes drug, you have an objective measure that you could use. You could say, "Okay, for diabetes, we wanna be able to reduce blood sugar." Or if you're going for a cancer drug: "We wanna reduce the size of a tumor." For pain there's really no biomarker, or objective measure, of pain. So researchers have to rely on *subjective* measures. I mean, we've all had to do that in the doctor's office–you know, those smiley faces to frowny faces or that 0 to 10 numerical scale: 0 being no pain, 10 being the worst pain imaginable. And so that subjectiveness of it is something that has made it really challenging to conduct these clinical trials.

And another thing that came up also that I hadn't really thought about when I talked to researchers about how hard it is is that there's just a really high bar. I mean, like you said, it's a nearly universal condition. Most of us are gonna encounter pain in our lives. And there's–so there's, what, 51 million people that have chronic pain, and that's not even counting postsurgical pain or temporary pain. And so there's a really high bar because if you're gonna give a medication, if it has side effects, even if it's just affecting a very small percentage of patients, that's gonna be a lot of people. So it has to be very, very safe.

And then one more thing about that, too, is effectiveness. I mean, there are opioids that have a lot of baggage, but they're also pretty effective, and they're generic at this point. They're pretty cheap. So there's a bar there as far as trying to come up with something that works as well as or better than opioids when you know opioids can be easily prescribed and are pretty cheap.

Feltman: Yeah, that makes sense. I mean, of course, given the concerns about, you know, the opioid epidemic, I'm sure a lot of people listening to this are very excited—I'm very excited at the prospect of a new class of pain medication. So what are the next steps? You know, how long is it, realistically, before people could be able to access these medications?

Broadfoot: So right now the FDA has granted priority review for the drug, and so it—it's looking at it, it was fast-tracked, and it should have a decision by January 2025. So it could be available next year for patients.

Feltman: Wow, that is a fast track for sure [laughs].

Broadfoot: [Laughs] Yeah, and I would note that the studies they conducted were and the *indication* that they're trying to get approval for is for acute pain. So they did these trials in patients that were undergoing surgery, so it's kind of this short-term, acute pain.

But chronic pain is really the bigger issue, potentially, and—you know, like I said, 51 million people deal with chronic pain; a lot of people are living with pain. And so they had done some studies earlier on—they had some phase 2 trials, and they're saying they're gonna launch phase 3 trials to look at the application of this drug in chronic pain—but that is kind of what everybody's most waiting for because that's where there is an even greater unmet need.

Feltman: Sure. Marla, thank you so much for coming on to chat with us. This was great.

Broadfoot: Yeah, this was lots of fun.

Rachel Feltman: That's all for today's episode. Tune in on Friday for the final installment of our Fascination miniseries on the hidden nature of math. This week, we'll be talking to some of the intrepid explorers who are discovering brand new math as we speak.

If you've got a few seconds to spare, leave us a rating and a review wherever you listen to podcasts. If your platform of choice allows you to subscribe or follow, it would be awesome if you could do that, too. It really helps other people find the show.

Science Quickly is produced by me, Rachel Feltman, along with Fonda Mwangi, Kelso Harper, Madison Goldberg and Jeff DelViscio. Shayna Posses and Aaron Shattuck fact-check our show. Our theme music was composed by Dominic Smith. Subscribe to *Scientific American* for more up-to-date and in-depth science news.

For *Scientific American*, this is Rachel Feltman. See you next time!

About the Authors

Rachel Feltman is former executive editor of Popular Science *and forever host of the podcast* The Weirdest Thing I Learned This Week. *She previously founded the blog* Speaking of Science *for the* Washington Post.

Marla Broadfoot is a freelance science writer who lives in North Carolina. She has a Ph.D. in genetics and molecular biology and is an adjunct at the University of North Carolina at Chapel Hill. Her feature on a new type of pain pill was published in our September 2024 issue.

Fonda Mwangi is an award-winning multimedia editor at Scientific American *and producer of* Science Quickly. *She previously worked at* Axios, *the* Recount *and* WTOP News. *She holds a master's degree in journalism and public affairs from American University in Washington, D.C.*

On the Horizon: Virtual Reality Therapy That Treats Chronic Pain

By Esther Hsieh

Strap on a headset, immerse yourself in an alternate reality and cure your pain—that's the idea of a recent study in Psychological Science.

Most people think of pain as something that happens in the body—I twist my head too far, and my neck sends a "pain signal" to the brain to indicate that the twisting hurts. In reality, pain is simply the brain telling us we are in danger. Although certain nerve endings throughout the body can indeed detect bodily harm, their signals are only one factor that the brain uses to determine if we should experience pain. Many cases of chronic pain are thought to be the result of obsolete brain associations between movement and pain.

To explore the mind's influence over pain, Daniel Harvie, a Ph.D. candidate at the University of South Australia, and his colleagues asked 24 participants who suffer from chronic neck pain to sit in a chair while wearing virtual-reality glasses and turn their head. The displays were manipulated to make the participants think that they were turning their head more or less than they actually were.

Subjects could swivel their head 6 percent more than usual if the virtual reality made them think they were turning less, and they could rotate 7 percent less than usual when they thought they were turning more.

The findings suggest that virtual-reality therapy has the potential to retrain the brain to understand that once painful movements are now safe, extinguishing the association with danger. Harvie believes that such therapy has the potential to restore full pain-free range of motion to people recovering from injuries and could perhaps help individuals with neurodegenerative diseases such as Parkinson's.

GLOSSARY

allodynia When something that isn't painful, such as a light touch, causes pain.

astrocytes Cells in the brain that support neurons, regulate blood flow, and manage communication between synapses in the body.

atrophy The wasting away or shrinking of muscle.

corticolimbic A system in the body that connects cognition and emotion and regulates behavior and emotional responses.

debilitating Something causing serious impairment that makes it hard to function normally.

desensitized To be indifferent or nonreactive to something.

ectopic Something out of place and not in their normal position in the body.

empathy The ability to understand someone's feelings, experiences, or thoughts.

indelible Something that's impossible to forget.

innocuous Something unlikely to cause injury.

interoception The sense of the internal state of the body, which allows awareness of hunger, thirst, respiration, heart rate, and other bodily needs.

intrinsic To be essential.

neuroplasticity The brain's ability to regorganize itself and form new neural connections.

pain chronification When pain transforms from temporary pain into chronic pain and lasts longer than normal healing time.

placebo effect When a person's mental or physical health improves after taking an inactive treatment.

postulate An idea that's assumed to be true without proof, often serving as a starting point for a theory.

psychopath A person with a personality disorder that's characterized by a lack of empathy and impulsive or antisocial behavior.

recalcitrant To be difficult to manage.

rheumatology A branch of medicine focused on diseases of the muscles, bones, joints, and connective tissues.

sociopath Someone with a mental health disorder that makes them disregard what is right and wrong and ignores the rights and feelings of others.

subliminal Messages that exist below conscious awareness.

FURTHER INFORMATION

Arcuri, Lauren. "The Physiology of Pain." American Physiological Society. March 2022. www.physiology.org/publications/news/the-physiologist-magazine/2022/march/the-physiology-of-pain?SSO=Y.

Armitage, Hanae. "Researchers Discover the Brain Cells that Make Pain Unpleasant." Stanford Medicine. January 17, 2019. med.stanford.edu/news/all-news/2019/01/researchers-discover-the-brain-cells-that-make-pain-unpleasant.html.

Broadfoot, Marla. "New Painkiller Could Bring Relief to Millions—Without Addiction Risk." *Scientific American*. August 20, 2024. www.scientificamerican.com/article/new-pain-medication-suzetrigine-prevents-pain-signals-from-reaching-brain/.

De Ridder, Divya Adhia, and Sven Vanneste. "The Anatomy of Pain and Suffering in the Brain and its Clinical Implications." *Science Direct*. August 19, 2021. www.sciencedirect.com/science/article/pii/S0149763421003560.

Farah, Troy. "Can Psychedelic Drugs Treat Physical Pain?" *Scientific American*. September 30, 2021. www.scientificamerican.com/article/can-psychedelic-drugs-treat-physical-pain/.

"'Ouch, that hurts!' The Science of Pain." *NIH Medline Plus Magazine*. May 23, 2023. magazine.medlineplus.gov/article/ouch-that-hurts-the-science-of-pain.

Pierre-Louis, Kendra, Fonda Mwangi, Alex Sugiura, and Naeem Amarsy. "The Surprising Science of Pain Can Help You Finally Feel Better." *Scientific American*. March 27, 2026. www.scientificamerican.com/podcast/episode/the-truth-about-pain-that-your-doctor-might-not-tell-you/.

Ribeiro, Celina. "The Fascinating Science of Pain—And Why Everyone Feels It Differently." *The Guardian*. July 13, 2025. www.theguardian.com/australia-news/2025/jul/14/

the-fascinating-science-of-pain-and-why-everyone-feels-it-differently.

Szalavitz, Maia. "A Recent Supreme Court Ruling Will Help People In Pain." *Scientific American*. September 19, 2022. www.scientificamerican.com/article/a-recent-supreme-court-ruling-will-help-people-in-pain/.

US Pain Foundation. "The Science of Understanding Pain." US Pain Foundation. October 27, 2025. uspainfoundation.org/pain-research-articles/the-science-of-understanding-pain/.

CITATIONS

1.1 The Science of Pain by Steve Mirsky (December 3, 2008); 1.2 The Chronification of Pain by Daniel Barron (December 29, 2017); 1.3 Nerve Damage Might Explain Chronic Pain by Stephani Sutherland (August 14, 2014); 1.4 New Culprits in Chronic Pain by R. Douglas Fields (November 1, 2009); 1.5 MIND on Pain: The Psychology of Pain by Howard L. Fields 1.6 The Battle over Pain in the Brain by Diana Kwon (September 1, 2009); 1.7 Is Pain a Construct of the Mind? by Stephen L. Macknik & Susana Martinez-Conde (September 1, 2013); 1.8 Neuroscientists Identify a Brain Signature of Pain by Michele Solis (September 1, 2013); 1.9 MIND on Pain: When Pain Lingers by Frank Porreca & Theodore Price (September 1, 2009); 1.10 Subliminal Messages Influence Our Experience of Pain by Simon Makin (September 1, 2015); 1.11 Does Financial Insecurity Lead to More Physical Pain? by Daisy Grewal (May 17, 2016); 2.1 MIND on Pain: Why People Experience Pain Differently by Ingrid Wickelgren (September 1, 2009); 2.2 It's Time To Rethink the Origins of Pain by Haider Warraich (September 8, 2022); 3.1 Why Headaches Remain One of Medicine's Most Misunderstood Disorders by Rachel Feltman, Fonda Mwangi, Alex Sugiura & Jeffery DelViscio (November 7, 2025); 3.2 Rising Physical Pain Is Linked to More 'Deaths of Despair' by Lucía Macchia (January 30, 2023); 3.3 The Mirror Cure for Phantom Pain by Lorimer Moseley (April 16, 2008); 4.1 Heal Your Injuries Faster than Ever by Lydia Denworth (January 20, 2026); 4.2 How Much Do Our Thoughts Shape Our Health? by Ellen Langer & Peter Aungle (May 3, 2024); 4.3 Learning to Accept Discomfort Could Help You Thrive by J. David Creswell (November 10, 2023); 5.1 Toward Better Pain Control by Allan Irwin Basbaum & David Julius (June 1, 2006); 5.2 Why the Pain Drug That Killed Prince Can Be Especially Dangerous by Stephani Sutherland (June 6, 2016); 5.3 What Is Journavx, the New Opioid-Free Painkiller from Vertex? by Allison Parshall (January 31, 2025); 5.4 Understanding Suzetrigine, a New Drug That Treats Pain at the Periphery by Rachel Feltman, Marla Broadfoot & Fonda Mwangi (October 2, 2024); 5.5 On the Horizon: Virtual Reality Therapy That Treats Chronic Pain by Esther Hsieh (July 1, 2015).

INDEX